THE POETRY GAMES: TRUTH OR DARE?

THE NORTH WEST

Edited By Daisy Job

First published in Great Britain in 2018 by:

Young Writers
Remus House
Coltsfoot Drive
Peterborough
PE2 9BF
Telephone: 01733 890066
Website: www.youngwriters.co.uk

FOREWORD

Welcome to 'The Poetry Games: Truth Or Dare? - The North West'.

For this Young Writers poetry competition we encouraged self-expression from secondary school pupils through a truth or dare format. The 'truth' entries reveal what the writer is passionate about, offer a sincere expression of their emotions or share their hopes, dreams and ambitions. The 'dare' entries are provocative in order to question the conventional and voice the writer's opinion; they may fight for their beliefs in verse or just tell a poetic tale of an audacious adventure.

We encouraged the writers to think about the technical aspects of their poems' compositions, whether they be an acrostic, haiku, free verse or another form, and to consider techniques such as metaphors, onomatopoeia, rhyme and imagery.

I'm so impressed with both the content and the style of the poems we received and I hope you enjoy them as much as I have. I'd like to congratulate all the writers who entered this competition and took up the challenge to join Team Truth or Team Dare.

Enjoy!

CONTENTS

Stretford High School, Stretford

Umar Nissar Hussain (13)	62
Malaeka Wahid (12)	64
Zac King (12)	66
Amir Sama (13)	67
Roman David Horne (12)	68
Mustafa Hafeji (12)	69
Laurence Ryan (12)	70
Shaniah McKenzie-Smith (12)	71

The Albion Academy, Salford

Alicia Carlon (11)	72
Noah Ros (14)	74
Christian Obialor (13)	76
Darcie Howard-Cahill (13)	78
Rukayat Yusuff (13)	80
Romi Mohamed (14)	82
Ellie Wild (13)	84
Connor Vaughan (11)	86
Amy Clayton (11)	87
Dieynaba Camara (14)	88
Laiba Shafique (14)	89
Ethan Alan Walsh (11)	90
Dillon Windsor (11)	91
Luke Joseph Paul Curtis (13)	92

Ullswater Community College, Penrith

Charlie Waistell (12)	93
Eleanor Harrison (11)	94
Holly Saward (11)	96
Allan Mason (11)	98
Morgana Isobell Grave (13)	101
Poppy Robertson (12)	102
Skye E Wohl (13)	104
Elinor Caitlin Hall (13)	106
Jenna Davidson (12)	108
Naomi Frost (13)	110
Charlotte Elliott (12)	112
Zoe Simpson (11)	114
Molly Jayne Scrivens (14)	116

Rachel Huschka (13)	118
Daisy Amber Robinson (12)	120
Lizzy Anne Hudspith-Spence (11)	121
Maisy Yates (13)	122
Alisha Chambers (13)	124
Martha Lynam (12)	126
Zara Young (13)	127
Poppy Carr (11)	128
Aimee Fowles (13)	129
Maddison Elliott (12)	130
Anna Victoria Hogg (12)	132
Olivia Armstrong (12)	134
Nicole Wallace (12)	135
Luke Coulston (13)	136
Alex (12) & Danny Lund (12)	138
Alice Rose Wade (11)	139
Danny Beaty (12)	140
Jasmine Keisha Bellas (11)	142
Liam Ludgate (11)	143
Emily Chambers (11)	144
Callum Popple (13)	145
Ellie Miller (13)	146
Millie Emma Bainbridge (11)	147
Joe Mortimer (11)	148
Jack Graham (13)	149
Arran Robert Gilpin (12)	150
Lillie Dixon (13)	151
Ella Harrison (11)	152
Erin Sowerby (13)	153
Ellie Chan (13)	154
Tom Nicholson (12)	155
Joshua Yerkess (11)	156
Hannah Louise Holmes (11)	157
Willan Jim Wallace (11)	158
Lottie Sharratt (12)	159
Isabel Sanderson (12)	160
Jack Wallace (11)	161
Annabel Murphy (14)	162
Samantha Anne Bufton (11)	163
Honey Railton (11)	164
Rhys Connor Akrigg (12)	165
Esmé Millie Fawcett (11)	166
Heather Mein (13)	167

Jessie Ridley (11)	168
Natasha Jade Malloy (11)	169
D'arcy Bell (12)	170
Joe Braithwaite (13)	171
Jack Wilson (11)	172
Rianna Harrison (11)	173
Danny Eland (11)	174
Reece Teasdale (11)	175
Tegan Mai Parkin (11)	176
Alfie Hay (11)	177
Elliot Baty (11)	178
Molly-Jane Guy-Gregg (11)	179
Rachel Abbott (11)	180
Ella Philips (11)	181
Charlie Southworth (12)	182
Jack Bowman (11)	183
Jessica Brown (12)	184
Josh Padgett (13)	185
Cody Robert Jackson (11)	186
Emily Mawson (11)	187
Matti Kowal (12)	188
Dominic Horrobin (12)	189
Ryan Carrick (13)	190
Morgan Goad (11)	191
Dominic Blenkharn (11)	192
Melissa Clark (11)	193
Sam Bayliffe (13)	194
Ella Hall (11)	195
Kira McDonald (11)	196
Keeley Thompson (14)	197
Tia Holly Emmens (13)	198
Katie Jade White (11)	199
Erin Dixon (11)	200
Lily Anne Kitching (14)	201
James Heape (11)	202
Aidan Powell-Currie (11)	203
Daniel Harrison (13)	204
Robbie Forsyth (13)	205
Kieran Eland (13)	206
Libby Burne (11)	207
Morgan Bland (11)	208
Mason McAneney (12)	209

Weatherhead High School, Wallasey

Safia Schulz (11)	210
Ellie Frost (12)	211
Hope Susan Lucas (12)	212

THE POEMS

HOMELESSNESS

Truth

This is what it feels like to be homeless...

Ouch! That was me being kicked in the leg again
As a woman bundled past me
Did she see me?
On her way into the office with her hot cup of coffee
Slam! The door shut behind her.

I am lying down in the cold, filthy doorway
What can I see?
Credit cards and cash in hand and sandwiches being bought
I will have a sausage sandwich and a cup of tea
It would make my day and fill me with glee.
Oh wait, I forgot no sausage sandwich or cup of tea for me
I don't think they would take cardboard boxes or plastic
cups as payment.

As the rest of my day slowly passes by,
I think back to when I was a busy office worker rushing by.
I wouldn't have stopped to look at people like me,
I felt no pity
Too busy thinking about my life to care
Now I know that no one chooses to be homeless.

Holly Charlotte Williams (12)
Alder Community High School, Hyde

MANKIND

Dare

Let's go back to the start,
The very very start,
Where the stegosaurus, supersaurus and strangely named
giants
Shattered the earth

There was no slaughter back then,
Only the food chain
There was no greed in those times,
Absolutely nothing was insane.

Evolution, evolution.

Rained down on the earth.
The Big Bang!
Hit 'em hard,
The next thing, the world's given birth.

The taste of ash,
Shh, the sound of silence.
Open your eyes...
The stone age is upon us, time to grow up,
Step through to bronze
Not gold, not silver.
You're losing the race to stay innocent and kind.
What a waste of mankind.

Iron age, Celts,
Search and search, you'll find
War has broken out, battles for greed, battles for hatred,
Battles for no reason. Only for the sight of treason.
What a waste of mankind.

Four centuries later,
Gladiators fought - *crash, wallop, kill!*
Citizens adore.
Entertainment to kill,
What's going on?
Saxons join the race.
Scotland's a place.
Vikings come next in quite a haste.

The rule of Henry VIII sent Britain in a whirl.
Remember, remember the fifth of November, gunpowder
used to try to blow up the pearl.
Time to put the past mistakes straight.
Queen Victoria.
Inventions, create.
Mills come around, send children to work.
Put a stop to this misery - What a waste of mankind.

World War I
World War II,
They fought for their country,
They fought for their king.
Many lives lost, many obscene.

Bow your head for honour, not for greed.
Thank you soldiers for planting a seed.

And right about now,
In the 21st Century
Terrorism. Murder. Fraud.
It is a rising issue.
It's a bit different from when dinosaurs roamed the earth.
And yes, we are still losing the race
To stay innocent and kind.
What a waste of mankind.

Faith Moore (11)
Alder Community High School, Hyde

POLLUTION, WHAT DOES IT DO?

Dare

Asthma, cancer and cardiovascular disease
Just a few effects of pollution I've seen.
Affecting all of us humans, animals too
We need a solution immediately, it's true.
Skin irritation, let's change this weather
Water pollution, it's apparent as ever.
'Oh no, I can't hear, it's stressing me out!'
All air pollution causing these droughts.
2012, the worst year in Nebraska
Pollution explains the melting ice in Alaska.

Leah-Ashley Norman (11)
Alder Community High School, Hyde

DREAM KEEPER

Truth

Sweet and beautiful child of mine,
Close your eyes and sleep tonight.
Sweet and beautiful child of mine,
Your dreams will take you far in flight.

Whatever happened to you today,
You'll relive again and again.
As you relive things will change,
In a spectacular sort of way!

Your cat's become a lion
Your feet will let you fly.
You're breathing underwater,
While leaping star to star at night.

I see it in your eyes my child,
These powers you have longed for.
So I grant you your wishes my child,
As I have done every night before.

Your dreams are calm and peaceful,
I protect them so you see
From the monsters at the back of your mind
Which every night break free.

I fight them off most nights my child,
Though they sometimes slip the gate
And end up in your dreams my child
To frighten you awake.

As dawn conquers night my child,
And the light seeps in your eyes.
You long so much to do it all again,
And pray for sunset to arrive.

Eva Byrne (11)
Alder Community High School, Hyde

DARING TO BE GOD

Dare

Mr Allkins thinks I'm reading but I'm not.
I'm daring to become God
Because I would be the most powerful person in existence
I would make another inhabitable plant in our solar system.

Mr Allkins thinks I'm writing but I'm not.
I'm daring to become a famous comedian
Because I like making people laugh
Over half the planet listen to my jokes every year on TV.

Mr Allkins thinks I'm working but I'm not.
I'm daring to act in a sci-fi comedy movie.
I would be the third most important character
I'm a villain, I'm trying to harvest rare resources on Mars.

Mr Allkins thinks I waste my time daydreaming,
But you see that's not the thing.
Today it might be just a dream,
But who dares to know what tomorrow will bring.

Matthew Rhys Cullen (12)
Clare Mount Specialist Sports College, Moreton

DANGEROUS DREAMS

Dare

Mr Allkins thinks I'm reading but I'm not.
I'm daring to climb up the tallest tower while it is raining
and lightning.
With all the slippery platforms it would be a slippery climb.

Mr Allkins thinks I'm writing but I'm not.
I'm daring to wander into the dangers of the killers trying to
escape the entity.
I would be fun and challenging, dying or surviving.

Mr Allkins thinks I'm working but I'm not.
I'm daring to get through the most broken and dangerous
bridge ever known to exist.
It would be hard but it would also be fantastic and shocking
to succeed.

Mr Allkins thinks I waste my time daydreaming,
But you see that's not the thing.
Today it might be just a dream,
But who dares to know what tomorrow will bring.

Callum Dawson (12)

Clare Mount Specialist Sports College, Moreton

DARING TO PLAY

Dare

Mr Allkins thinks I'm reading but I'm not.
I'm daring to be a professional footballer and play at
Wembley.
I'm going to score the winning goal.

Mr Allkins thinks I'm writing but I'm not.
I'm daring to play a game of football with Cristiano
Ronaldo.
I want to be a better player with the best player in the world
and legend.

Mr Allkins thinks I'm working but I'm not.
I'm daring to spend a day with the players of Everton and
lead them out at their new stadium.
I'll sit with the players on the bench and watch them win.

Mr Allkins thinks I waste my time daydreaming,
But you see that's not the thing.
Today it might be just a dream,
But who dares to know what tomorrow will bring.

Alfie Harrison (12)
Clare Mount Specialist Sports College, Moreton

DARING TO SKYDIVE

Dare

Mr Allkins thinks I'm reading but I'm not.
I'm daring to skydive off the biggest building in the world.
A lot of air is going through my hair.

Mr Allkins thinks I'm writing but I'm not.
I'm daring to swim in some melted snow in a scuba mask.
It feels like I'm going to freeze into an ice block!

Mr Allkins thinks I'm working but I'm not.
I'm daring to tackle a rhino off the school building.
It is really funny and I can't stop laughing.

Mr Allkins thinks I waste my time daydreaming,
But you see that's not the thing.
Today it might be just a dream,
But who dares to know what tomorrow will bring.

Sam Vaughan (12)
Clare Mount Specialist Sports College, Moreton

DAYDREAMING

Dare

Mr Allkins thinks I'm reading but I'm not.
I'm daring to ride my bike on a summer morning.
The summer breeze is going through my hair.

Mr Allkins thinks I'm writing but I'm not.
I'm daring to jump off the tallest building in the world (with a parachute).
I'll be going faster than a cheetah!

Mr Allkins thinks I'm working but I'm not.
I'm daring to beat Usain Bolt in the 200 metre sprint.
AKA I am pretty fast.

Mr Allkins thinks I waste my time daydreaming,
But you see that's not the thing.
Today it might be just a dream,
But who dares to know what tomorrow will bring.

Frankie Spargo (12)
Clare Mount Specialist Sports College, Moreton

DARING TO DREAM

Dare

Mr Allkins thinks I'm reading but I'm not.
I'm daring to be Nathan Drank from the Unchartered
Games.
I'm finding treasure.

Mr Allkins thinks I'm writing but I'm not.
I'm daring to travel to a deserted island full of attractive
women.
I'm lying back with a drink in my hand.

Mr Allkins thinks I'm working but I'm not.
I'm daring to take a holiday to Greece.
I'm watching the sunset glisten on the water.

Mr Allkins thinks I waste my time daydreaming,
But you see that's not the thing.
Today it might be just a dream,
But who dares to know what tomorrow will bring.

Elliot Chisholm (12)
Clare Mount Specialist Sports College, Moreton

MR ALLKINS THINKS I'M READING, BUT I'M NOT...

Dare

Mr Allkins thinks I'm reading but I'm not.
I'm daring to go to Spain,
I am watching Real Madrid play football.

Mr Allkins thinks I'm writing but I'm not.
I'm daring to go to America,
I'm going on the arcades.

Mr Allkins thinks I'm working but I'm not.
I'm daring to go to Liverpool
I'm going to cheer on Everton at Anfield.

Mr Allkins thinks I waste my time daydreaming,
But you see that's not the thing.
Today it might be just a dream,
But who dares to know what tomorrow will bring.

Michael Coathup (13)
Clare Mount Specialist Sports College, Moreton

MR ALLKINS THINKS I'M READING, BUT I'M NOT...

Dare

Mr Allkins thinks I'm reading but I'm not.
I'm daring to go on an aeroplane and sit next to my mum.

Mr Allkins thinks I'm writing but I'm not.
I'm daring to go to the shops and the cinema to buy toys
and see Dirty Dancing.

Mr Allkins thinks I'm working but I'm not.
I'm daring to go to the pet shop to buy a dog and call her
Tilly.

Mr Allkins thinks I waste my time daydreaming,
But you see that's not the thing.
Today it might be just a dream,
But who dares to know what tomorrow will bring.

Georgia Gill (13)
Clare Mount Specialist Sports College, Moreton

FAMILY

Truth

This is to our family
The ones who watched us grow.
The people who made us happy
When we were feeling low.

To the ones who taught us to walk and talk
And the ones that taught us to throw.
The ones who took us to our first game
Even if we were a pain.

The ones who came to watch our show
And clapped at the end
Even if they didn't know what it was.

The people who showed us how to ride a bike
And helped us fly our first kite.
So this poem is for the ones who have helped us in life.

Reeve Christall (15)
Clare Mount Specialist Sports College, Moreton

MR ALLKINS THINKS I'M READING, BUT I'M NOT...

Dare

Mr Allkins thinks I'm reading but I'm not.
I'm daring to go to St Chad's to play on the Wii.

Mr Allkins thinks I'm writing but I'm not.
I'm daring to play games on my iPad at home.

Mr Allkins thinks I'm working but I'm not.
I'm daring to go home to see my mum and my dog Honey.

Mr Allkins thinks I waste my time daydreaming,
But you see that's not the thing.
Today it might be just a dream,
But who dares to know what tomorrow will bring.

Imogen Rowe (13)
Clare Mount Specialist Sports College, Moreton

MR ALLKINS THINKS I'M READING, BUT I'M NOT...

Dare

Mr Allkins thinks I'm reading but I'm not.
I'm daring to go on holiday and cruise around.

Mr Allkins thinks I'm writing but I'm not.
I'm daring to move house and decorate the back garden.

Mr Allkins thinks I'm working but I'm not.
I'm daring to play FIFA 18 with my friends.

Mr Allkins thinks I waste my time daydreaming,
But you see that's not the thing.
Today it might be just a dream,
But who dares to know what tomorrow will bring.

Callum Bartlett (13)
Clare Mount Specialist Sports College, Moreton

MR ALLKINS THINKS I'M READING, BUT I'M NOT...

Dare

Mr Allkins thinks I'm reading but I'm not.
I'm daring to go to France.

Mr Allkins thinks I'm writing but I'm not.
I'm daring to go swimming with my family.

Mr Allkins thinks I'm working but I'm not.
I'm daring to be at home with my dog, Monty.

Mr Allkins thinks I waste my time daydreaming,
But you see that's not the thing.
Today it might be just a dream,
But who dares to know what tomorrow will bring.

Esme Cotton (13)
Clare Mount Specialist Sports College, Moreton

THE POWER WE TAKE

Truth

The power we take for our life is another person's future life.
The footsteps behind me.
Every night I see her
She never misses a night
I think it is my conscience trying to say something
I regret what I have done
We were such a perfect couple
I never meant to hurt you
But you had no time for me
But I will be meeting up with you soon
Don't worry.

Mollie Parry (14)
Clare Mount Specialist Sports College, Moreton

MILKSHAKES MAKE ME HAPPY

Truth

Milkshakes make me happy
The creamy, creamy taste
My favourite is strawberry
Perfect with a doughnut
So Krispy Kreme is the place to go.

Ben Thompson (15)
Clare Mount Specialist Sports College, Moreton

TURING

Truth

Once I was a hero
Battled the chaos of letters and numbers
Participated in the world's worst wars
All behind closed doors.

Hidden in the darkroom
Of the sheltered house
I made magic out of metal
To solve problems that wouldn't settle.

But they will never know what I have done.
Glory goes to the truly brave
I am just another face
In a crowded place.

Fighting a secret
That wounds your life
Of the very worst kind
The war of the mind.

A childhood of tears
One person knew of my pain
Locked away in a cupboard
A deep desire longed to be explored.

The mind is just a machine
It computes, it deciphers
Can solve the most challenging puzzles
But under the burden of emotions it buckles.

They solved my cipher
Untangled the ugly truth
Of a beautiful love
That I saved for you.

You - who stood beside me
When no one else would
I gave you my heart
'Til death do us part.

I built my life on a lie
Secret meetings, secret persona
That all crumbled and caved in
Due to my love for 'sin'.

They will never know what I have done.
They didn't care
That they owed me their life
They only wanted to see me under the knife.

They poisoned my mind
Bleached me their bland colours
This is one problem no matter what
I will always be lost.

I can no longer find the solution.
Criminality clings to me in chains
What did I do in the war?
I don't care anymore.

All I have left is the shrapnel of life
For now the grand curtain is drawn aside
But this is who I am
I can no longer lie.

They say an apple a day
Will keep the doctors away.

Did Snow White have the answer?
A peaceful sleep with only one bite
In her heart she held the happiness
To the darkness of the world

I say goodnight.

Olivia Senior
Cronton Sixth Form College, Widnes

I HEAR AMERICA CRYING

Truth

My eyes close with the burden of the dead.
A tear for the fifty-eight, now cold.
'Condolences for the victims,' he said.

A right to bear arms washes their rivers red.
What so proudly they hail turns man to mould.
Eyes have closed with the burden of the dead.

What will be woken to next, I greatly dread.
Two hundred and seventy this year has known -
'Condolences for the victims,' he says.

They killed the first and made their misplaced bed -
A land of freedom built on blood and bones.
Our eyes close with the burden of the dead.

Nobodies in their capes made of bloodshed,
Galvanised, in history their stories told.
'Condolences for the victims,' he said.

The star-spangled banner that flies ahead,
Atop mangled bodies that lie below.
Our eyes close with the burden of the dead.
'Condolences for the victims,' is all he said.

Jack Radford
Cronton Sixth Form College, Widnes

HE NEVER LISTENED

Dare

'It wasn't my fault,' I murmur,
The blackened eyes of justice were trained on me like a
sniper scope
My blackened eyes were trained on my broken hand.
They needed someone to blame. A finger to point.
So instead of protection,
I am demonised.
Golden hair stained red with lust.
Green eyes the shade of envy.
The purple of my bruises doesn't get mentioned.
'He wouldn't listen,' I say
Picking at the foreign skin under my nails.
I remember I had them nicely painted for Him,
Burgundy, His favourite colour.
Never liked it myself,
But what he says, goes.
No. What he said.
I achieved my freedom when they shackled my hands.
Though the sandy brown dotting my skin reminds me of His
eyes
And the shape of His hands are stitched into my skin.
A ghost can't do much to the living,
His hands can't reach me from Hell.

'I did say no,' I grin
A missing tooth in my smile
'I always said no,
But he never listened.'

Jenny Preece
Cronton Sixth Form College, Widnes

THE MIRROR OF LIFE

Dare

In the mirror of life there is wealth, there is anguish.

On one side, a child wakes up warm and cosy,
In a bed free of worries, lying on aspirations and dreams,
Awakened by the soft caressing of a mother's hand,
Awakened by love.
Awakened with freedom.

Now look into the mirror.
Look harder.

On the other side, a child wakes up cold and wet,
In a room filled with disease, filled with regret,
She is awakened by the rough grip of an unknown arm,
Awakened by the sound of gunshots and screams,
Awakened by violence.
Awakened with fear.

Yesterday, she wanted ponies,
Today, she cried for dolls,
And tomorrow, she'll beg for candy.

But, yesterday she wanted sleep,
Today, she cried for them to stop,
And tomorrow, she'll beg for freedom.

Both born into the same world,
Yet on different sides of the mirror.

Molly Raby (17)
Cronton Sixth Form College, Widnes

THE SECRET OF SOCIETY

Truth

Faces. Blank faces consumed by the devil that ensnares us
all.
Nothing in complaint; nobody dares speak up.
Confused.
Why can't we wake up?
The secret: we are blinded by the normality of what should
be unacceptable.
The normality that we treat friends like foes because we
cannot tell the
difference anymore.
Was it ever an oddity?
Once.
Once upon a time people didn't ignore others, kindness spilt
from hearts like
the blood that now flows from our actions and words.
The secret: this time never honestly existed.
Only a fable.
A fable of goodwill, honesty and trust that has been weaved
by demons since
the beginning of time.
But those demons are not monsters or plagues or famines.
The secret: we are the demons.
And the secret is killing us all.

Emma Butler

Cronton Sixth Form College, Widnes

116 123

Dare

Twine these vines through
Twisting fingers, morning
Glories into moon singers

This season is growing short

Plant the seeds, rose petals
Under violet skin, give me scent,
An identity, I'm growing thin

This season is growing short

Paint me blue and yellow
Happy and sad, wrap the cord
Today I'm getting mad

This season is growing short

Watch me from the window
Do not move an inch, cut me open,
It's time for the lynch

This season is growing short

Burrow me deep, pull out
The roots, barrel to the head,
Man the gun and shoot

This season has grown short.

Lucy Jayne Tasker (17)
Cronton Sixth Form College, Widnes

I'M FINE

Dare

They surround you.
The happiness suffocating.
The demons suffocate.
'You look tired'
I'm fine.
Insomnia,
an illness.
Sleepless nights.
Stressful days.
'Restless night'
I'm fine
The darkness.
Itching to escape.
The demons they take over.
Never to escape.
'Are you sure you're fine?'
I'm fine
Deathly pale.
The absence of colour.
Nothing but flesh and bones.
'You look sick...'
I'm fine
The cold hands of death.
Caught in its grasp.

Something reaches in.
The darkness gone.
The light seeps through.
Curtains open.
The heat of the sun burns your skin.
The morning sun rose.
Vanquishing shadows.
'How are you feeling today?'
I'm... getting better
She was there.
Your saviour.
The colour to your black and white world.
'I'm getting better.'

Amy Pye
Cronton Sixth Form College, Widnes

THE TORMENTOR

Dare

They say that everything happens for a reason,
But whoever made that statement should be sent down for treason.
Temptation is a void you can't help but fall in,
But then you wonder why the consequences are calling.
Is karma the culprit of losing the ones we love?
Is it why rain chooses to plummet from above?
She torments you, leaves you paranoid, catches you from behind, and begins the void...

Karma is an occasion that won't follow a diary,
It will ambush you like a soldier in an army.
But don't assume that she will apologise,
It's her priority to make sure your pain will maximise.
So to you who are willing to play with fire,
Be warned that you'll only strengthen her desire.
She torments you, leaves you paranoid,
Catches you from behind, and begins the void...

But at the same time they want you to live life to the fullest,
But how can I please the punisher without my life being the dullest?
She torments me, leaves me paranoid,
Catches me from behind, and begins the void...

Rose Whewell (11)
Fallibroome Academy, Macclesfield

 DARE

THE VOICES OF CHOICES

Dare

What's that voice inside your head?
Your conscience or the devil?
Dreams or decisions?
Your most secret desires
Or maybe something else...?

Who was your first true love?
Have you ever ripped a foxglove?
What's your deepest, darkest secret?
Tell me all your bad side,
I dare you!

I dare you to hit her,
I'll get trouble,
I don't care!

Stay up all night,
I'll try with all my might,
We'll have a midnight feast,
Until the night has ceased!
Are you sure I won't turn into a beast?
Of course not, don't be a cheat!

Annabel Rose Axcell (13)
Fallibroome Academy, Macclesfield

IT

Truth

Controlling, that's what it is,
You are the puppet controlled by strings,
It is the master pulling at your strings,
It has captured you,
Trapping you with a prison cell of thoughts,
The thoughts are its weapon,
Hypnotising your mind to think you are a failure.

But part of you knows that isn't true,
That part of you knows that it is your bully,
No one can see it,
No one can find it,
Only you can hear it,
Loud and clear,
Only you know what tricks it plays on you,
Tricking your mind,
Making you feel worried and sad,
Forcing you to do actions to get rid of those emotions,
It torments you,
But only you know how to defeat it.

It may be trapping you now,
But slowly you will be able to escape,
You will have ups and downs but that's all right,

Soon it will be harmless,
Soon you will be happy,
Your mind will be calm,
You mind will be at ease,
It caused this,
It made you a mindful person,
It is anxiety.

Amar Kaur Bassi (14)
Fallibroome Academy, Macclesfield

THE REGRET IN ME

Truth

Like a plague it infects the body,
Heart, soul and mind,
The one time I was left unscripted,
The sparks began to fly,
Unconsciously I feel the call of anger,
Clasp me in its jaws,
I cry out for help,
But the thorns and petals rip me apart,
Like a good and evil war,
But the prick of a flame burns inside,
But suddenly extinguished once more,
Pain runs deep but regret runs deeper,
My soul ripped apart not once, but twice,
The psychological pain working inside,
The brain clicking like clockwork,
As much as I hate this feeling,
I know I must forgive myself.

Grace Holly Ainscough (12)
Fallibroome Academy, Macclesfield

WHAT I DID WRONG

Dare

I looked around sadly at my ruined home,
at my parents, crying as they were restrained by the guards.
I climbed inside the prison cart and remained silent,
knowing with every breath I took I was a second closer to
her end.
I hung my head, refusing to meet my executioner's eyes.
There before me, people booed and hissed.
I felt an emptiness.
It wasn't meant to end like this, I had much more to give.
I was forced to the ground, the axe raised,
I turned and whispered,
"You will remember me,
not in your dreams, but your nightmares!"

Hannah Boardman

Fallibroome Academy, Macclesfield

NIGHTFALL

Truth

When a relationship dies was it ever alive?
When it started, was it magic?
Did it once gleam with joy?
It's funny how someone can change your heart like, three,
two, one, destroy!
When you thought you were safe from that desolate feeling,
When you wake up and remember you were only dreaming.
We all have flaws though we can't always see,
Roses have thorns
And bees, they sting.
If your relationship hurts, then why hold on?
It will only get worse as night breaks dawn.

Love is like a crystal, shattered by the nightfall.

Rebekah Boardman (12)
Fallibroome Academy, Macclesfield

THE REASON WHY

Truth

Does life always have to come to an end?
People make you think that it is just around the bend.
With even more causes of death nowadays,
The freedom of life hides in the haze.
A girl who wants to live forever:
To do this she will have to be clever.
She should make the most out of life,
Behave and never strife.
She will cherish all loved ones,
Then watch them pass on.
She carried on living
And that's the very reason why,
She didn't live forever, nor did she die.

Evie Eddie (12)

Fallibroome Academy, Macclesfield

THIS TIME OF HATRED

Truth

Bullies are despicable,
But don't blame it on them.
It's not always their fault,
They could have been taught to do wrong,
What happens in their life no one knows.

As a person who has been bullied,
And also who was a bystander,
I know first hand that it hurts,
It hurts so much that you get lost in the dark.

I'm here to tell you, to hold on tight,
Bullies have reasons for what they do,
Be it their fault or others,
It still doesn't mean that you have to scribble and scream.

Come out of the dark,
Come one, come all,
This time of hatred has to fall,
There are other ways to see the truth,
Turn to your friends,
They know the real you.

Gwen Springall (13)
Great Sankey High School, Great Sankey

STEREOTYPE

Dare

Is stereotype even a thing? Of course it is!
What if my friend who is a boy wants to dance and sing?
Is this wrong or is this right?
Why should he have to fight?
Why can't he dance and twirl
Without them calling him a girl?
Why can't they leave him alone
Instead of recording him on their phone?
So, he's not a stereotypical lad
That doesn't mean he's sad
So dance and sing all day long
Sing it loud and sing it strong.

Melissa Watson (12)
Great Sankey High School, Great Sankey

I AM

Truth

I am gullible,
I am weird,
I am loud,
I am crazy,
As well as mental.

But I am also,
Helpful and
I am kind,
I am intelligent,
I am enthusiastic.

I am all of these things,
As well as much more.
With my brown hair,
Blue eyes and pale skin
I look like an average girl,

But I am so much more.
I have my likes,
I have my dislikes,
I have my favourite things,
But some are extraordinary.

I like to dance but,
I also like the supernatural.
I dislike football but,
I also dislike cats.
I am Amy.

Amy Jayne Brown (14)
Great Sankey High School, Great Sankey

SKELETONS

Dare

If humans were just skeletons and all looked the same,
Would we judge and cause so much pain?
Or if I were blind and could not see,
Would I judge them the way they judged me?
Would we see hearts or brains or personality?
Instead of spots and weight and things that shouldn't
matter in reality.
So if we were all skeletons and all looked the same,
I suspect we could be set free again.

Katie Roberts (12)
Great Sankey High School, Great Sankey

TODAY'S SOCIETY

Dare

Billionaires,
Millionaires,
Money, money, money,
All everybody thinks,
All everybody wants,
Money, money, money.
Economic growth,
Increasing GDP,
Have we forgotten
About the old times?
Social gatherings,
Family meet-ups,
Technology has taken over,
In this day and age,
In this society,
Money, money, money.

Jake Bratherton (14)
Great Sankey High School, Great Sankey

THE LAST PIECE OF DIRT

Dare

New lives
The last piece of dirt
Hits my cold, sour skin;
A piece of wood hammered down on my coffin.
The last drop of rain descends on the ground;
You won't find God in this crowd.
Time is up.

Everything seems to be clear;
New skin, new body and hair;
Everything is new and bright;
Wait - is this life?

I eat and drink whilst time flows
I go to school and much more
SATs and GCSE out of the way
Once a child now an adult

But then I get older unlike before
Grey hair with lots more
A walking stick and children run all around me
I see a beautiful woman, old and wrinkly
She stands beside me

Then sorrow slaps me in the face
The last piece of dirt smacked my skin
A piece of wood went above me
The last drop fell before me
A loud thud and it was all gone
Was I going to carry on or end up in Heaven?

New skin and fur and little tiny legs
Green and hungry for a crunchy leaf
I'm suddenly in a cocoon and hatch with a shine
Long bright wings with a designed pattern
Can't fly but can feel myself flutter
Big antlers and little legs
Then I realised I was something different than a human
Yes I'm a butterfly

Is this true
Or did I experience life for the third time?

Zakib Sardar (12)

Manchester Academy, Moss Side

I AIN'T PERFECT

Truth

I ain't perfect
Why do you think this is OK?
You torment me with names like lizard skin
Does it look like I am an animal?

I got a comment this one time saying that
My skin was beautiful,
Why can't everyone be like that?
She said that it was a piece of art.
That really warmed my heart

No I ain't perfect but I'm human after all
These things you call me, they hurt me real bad
They make me real mad, man.

I'll repeat this again - it hurts real bad.
Look at perception,
This form of expression
Is this depression or oppression?
What is your obsession?
That's just an idea of what has been sent to me
You really seem to have no clue and you will never see

This really seems like I have fallen to the ground
Ground breaking, ground shaking
What am I making, you ask?

I'm trying to tell you that I may
Not be perfect but I'm still a human being

This ain't my downfall, this is my rise from the shadows
I'm gonna do what is right and talk about it, not have a
fight!

Chris Thananki (13)
Manchester Academy, Moss Side

EQUALITY IS A MYTH

Dare

I can't drive
I can't walk freely without being accompanied by a man
I can't get an education
Who am I?

I can't enjoy certain things without being called 'feminine' or
'metrosexual'
I can't show emotion or cry because it's not 'manly'
I can't confess what my wife did to me, society will
emasculate me.
Who am I?

I can't love who I want without being executed or
imprisoned
I can't come out without criticism, not only to my family but
society too
I can't wear what I want because it doesn't match my
'gender'
Who am I?

You've heard about my struggle, have you ever helped me?
You walk amongst me every day, why do your eyes bore into
me?
I'm not sorry for who I am, because, candidly, why should I
be?

You know who I am -
Don't pretend you don't see me.

Ibrahim Mohammad (13)

Manchester Academy, Moss Side

I DARE YOU

Dare

Deep in the depths of your everlasting mind,
Lurks a thing you may never find.
It plays with you, it hurts you, and it stirs up your emotion,
It takes all power off you just like a potion.

Now here I am revealing to you,
What I preach about.
The truth is discovered by only a few,
But it's time you find out.

Destiny, that is the word, that is all you need,
To go and chase your future, to go and chase your dreams.
So I dare you to grab your chance and *not* throw it away,
Because you will regret the choices, the choices you have
made.

Cheryl Babu Thananki (11)

Manchester Academy, Moss Side

UNTITLED

Dare

Life and death
Back from what seemed like a hellhole,
Back here again.
Living my life.
Not death; as that's what it seemed like.
Down there in the inferno,
It screamed in my ear,
It made me want to hate,
All it made me think of -
Is that we're in a game of life and death.

What was I supposed do?
Sit there and die over and over again?
Let them tear me apart?
I wasn't going to play their game,
The game of life and death.
It was beyond a game -
It decided your fate.
The devil's sinister sneer.

Haleem Abed (12)
Manchester Academy, Moss Side

UNTITLED

Dare

Suicide.
It's a fear.
Our mind asks us 'Why are we even here?'
It brings families to tears.

People are making assumptions about the next terror attack,
But they don't focus on the current things.
Suicide and distraught feelings.

Insecurities, hatred, stress.
That's all we've got on our minds.
Everyone pointing fingers,
They can never be kind.

You don't know their story,
You don't know mine.
Don't bully people,
It isn't fine.

Natasha Rahman (12)
Manchester Academy, Moss Side

IS THIS A LIE OR TRUTH? DARE YOU

Dare

Is this a lie?
Or is it truth.
Is this how it works?
Or is it a manipulation too.

We do anything, every day,
Whatever they say,
Even if it's not A OK,
We do it anyway.

What is school?
Who makes up the rules?
The one who tells the teachers what to do?
To teach us what to believe?
And what to see?

Is this right?
Or is it corrupt?
Should we be taught this?
Or something else.
Is this how it works.
Or is it a manipulation too.
Is this how it works?

Hamza Hagi
Manchester Academy, Moss Side

UNTITLED

Dare

I wake up in my grave
All I see is my cut head
All I remember is me running from my sister's grave
I was just an unlucky slave
They caught me and stabbed me
Who am I supposed to be?
Is it life or death?
I remember it was the game of truth or dare
I took dare
It was beyond a game
There was no fame
It decided your fate
Become a slave
Or live in a grave
Take all your life
And cut with a sharp knife
My life cannot be put back together
My sister... Heather.

Abdirahman Sadeeq (11)
Manchester Academy, Moss Side

DETERIORATING SOCIETY

Truth

Because I'm gay
Because I'm straight
Resentment towards me making me feel pain
Melancholy possesses my veins
My feminine walk
My feminine talk
My feminine gestures
You lambaste my looks
Leaving me shook
I want to draw on my arm
Would you concern yourself to my exit of life or would you
persist in continuing the hate...even though I'm gone?

Monyah Moigboi (13)
Manchester Academy, Moss Side

LIFE WILL BE LIFE

Truth

Life will be life.
Life is a challenge,
That we're still yet to figure out,
Because we still have doubt,
It's a problem that we're still yet to figure out.

In life we will scream and shout,
But then we'll go about,
We have love and we have hate,
And we will always have a mate.

Yolanda Hardy-Bailey (12)
Manchester Academy, Moss Side

FRIENDLESS

Truth

F eeling lonely
R emembering my old friends
I need someone to talk to
E ven a teacher
N o one cares
D o look at me
L ove doesn't hurt
E veryone walks past
S earching for a friend
S omeone listen

Elle Louise Frith (12)
St Hilda's CE High School, Sefton Park

AGEING

Dare

As young children we would think and ponder,
With much anticipation,
If life would get easier as we get older,
That everything would be better if we were taller,
No responsibility or obligation.

As we mature it's not like it first seemed,
Becoming more nervous and anxious,
Not as fun as we originally dreamed,
Having to seek others' sanctions.

Realising as we become less naïve,
More knowledgeable and our minds easier to conceive
That we may not achieve our dreams,
Not without hard work and perspiration
With our grades reaching escalation.

As nostalgia grows with passing years,
Looking back with fondness,
It seems that we can face our fears,
Feeling warmth and gladness.

Maturity can give us different opportunities,
Although we are more stressed,
Further accountable for our actions,

We can at least look back and say we've made progress,
And aspire to our goals which we'll celebrate with
satisfaction.

Umar Nissar Hussain (13)
Stretford High School, Stretford

NO BULLY!

Truth

A bully is a boy or a girl
Who makes you feel sad,
Who says or does things,
That make you feel bad.

A bully may laugh,
When you make a mistake,
Or when they call you names,
Or push you, shove you or shake.

What do you do,
When you're bullied today?
Just stay calm,
And walk away!

Go and tell a grown up,
They'll know what to do,
Teachers and parents you trust,
Are there to help you.

What if you see
A bully pick on your friend?
How do you make the bully
Come to an end?

Tell the bully to stop!
Go find a grown up,
They will understand.

The world should be a safe place,
To explore, love and stay,
If you speak up and stand up,
The bullies won't get away!

Malaeka Wahid (12)
Stretford High School, Stretford

INSIDE OF ME

Dare

It was written down in prophecy
About war and such atrocity,
Nations rise against a nation
Causing wrath and reprobation.

From a world designed through love
By its maker up above,
Mankind's greed and selfish power
Seeks to pillage and devour.

Is there hope amidst the trouble
That can curb and burst the bubble
Of destruction and deception?
I think not upon reflection.

There's no answer in religion,
Once a statue, now a pigeon.
What can set our planet free
Must begin inside of me.

Zac King (12)
Stretford High School, Stretford

THE GAME

Dare

Football is not just a game,
It can put people into the spotlight,
It can light them up like a flame,
Which can also cause a fight.

Football is about pride,
It is about playing for your team,
It can be a fun ride,
Where you live out your dream.

Football is a thing of beauty,
It is the player's biggest duty,
It is a thing you can't forget,
And definitely,
You won't regret!

Amir Sama (13)
Stretford High School, Stretford

MY BIKE

Dare

Riding my bike
The thing that I like
Helmet has a spike
But sometimes it is a hike.

Wheels made of steel,
Handlebars have a good feel,
Bought from a man called Neil,
I hope they don't peel.

My bike is green,
People say it is obscene,
But I am very keen,
Made just for a teen.

I will always take care of my bike
Because riding my bike is the thing that I like.

Roman David Horne (12)
Stretford High School, Stretford

BULLYING

Dare

Why does bullying occur
Who shall dare hit a child
What can we do?

Words can hurt and make you sad
Even if you've not done anything bad
And all they'll say is, 'That's rad!'

Words can hurt and make you feel blue
They make me take time off school for a fake flu
You may think you're cool
But just keep in mind that you're a fool.

Mustafa Hafeji (12)
Stretford High School, Stretford

SLAVERY

Dare

S o many innocent people dead

L ots of agony

A ggressive owners

V ery poor hygiene

E very slave beaten

R eally cruel punishments

Y ou will not go through the amount of pain slaves had to go through.

Laurence Ryan (12)

Stretford High School, Stretford

EVERYBODY HAS A NAME

Dare

Everybody has a name
Some are different
Some are the same
Some are short
Some are long
All are right
None are wrong
My name is Shaniah
It is special to me
It's exactly who
I want to be.

Shaniah McKenzie-Smith (12)
Stretford High School, Stretford

I MISS YOU MUM

Truth

I miss you Mum:
Who's going to tuck me in tonight?
Who's going to scare away my fright?
Who's going to stop them bullying me?
Who's going to make me a delicious tea?
Because as the days pass by,
All they do is make me cry.

Tonight I'll gather clothes to keep me warm,
But that's not enough, my heart's still torn,
I want to go back to when you were here
Because I'd make a wish that you would never disappear.
Just one more wish,
Just one more kiss,
I wish I could say goodbye
But that's too late, time has passed by.
Under this roof, I don't feel safe
But all I need is a little bit of faith.

The walls are closing in on me,
I'm finding it really hard to see
Because my eyes are filling up with tears,
Because I've been alone for years and years.
I call your name but you never answer.

My dreams won't come, I just want to be a dancer,
But we can't afford it because we're too poor.
I've tried to earn money by doing a chore
Like sewing and cleaning and much, much more.
But now I know you're not going to come back
Because when you left, you didn't even pack.

Alicia Carlon (11)
The Albion Academy, Salford

AND THEN THE OCEAN WILL STIR

Dare

A sailor is cast out into the harsh waves
A float is crafted from a single thought,
But where did this apparition come from
This blessed spirit... thought... story?
Ink runs through its veins like currents on the seabed
This float built with soft hands and deep pouches.
Our God's wisdom for people,
Sandy-coloured like the seabed itself.

Until the tide of time changes; people
Now preach for everyone - light and dark skin
Dark skin - earthy like the ground that provides
Where we will go after our wise judgements
A rule of the ocean is that water will flow
And then crash, yet forward it goes.

The water spits, stirs and gurgles at the shores of Britain
And from this sound across the expanse, cries can be heard
'How beautiful the boat is. Why do we tarnish it with our
monotonous alterations?
Why do we stab with our penknives at this paper boat?
If it was wrong then, why now is it right?
What's written is written.'

And when the ocean is still, foam settles
In the depths of the past the float halts...
Our voyage to our heaven over a faint haze...
The sailor is cast out into the waves once again.

Noah Ros (14)
The Albion Academy, Salford

UNTITLED

Dare

You hide the truth
You control the world by your decision.
You're regarded to be higher than us
But we share the same values.
We're all humans.
Yet you shape our mindset like clay
You based your decisions on money you'll pay.

We are raised to be independent
Yet our beliefs aren't ours.
We speak your words.

We're punished for speaking publicly
The truth and our mind
We are trapped in your world.

We are sponges,
We soak in all our experiences and our views
By why own our human body
And not have the right to control it to its fullest?

Conspiracies and coincidences
Making us struggle to understand what to believe.
You hide the truth.

Locked in a black place
Identity unknown with no trace
I see sunlight from a mile away
I run,
I run,
I run.
Yet I'm still here.
I cry and begin to fear
I tilt my head up and realise I'm near
I helplessly walk further and
I see life
I see green,
I see water,
I see ice.
I am free.

Christian Obialor (13)
The Albion Academy, Salford

LABELLED

Truth

We are brought up in a society
Which tells us right from wrong,
Multicoloured hair, piercings?
We are the freaks.
Big, bright eyes; bleached blonde hair?
We must be fake
Braces, glasses, smart?
We are labelled 'The Nerds'.
But they all have one thing in common
They are labelled.

From the day we paint our nails
Or put gel in our hair, or even ask for our first lipstick
We are turned into horrible monsters.
We are praised for the money
And expense covering our fragile, ugly bodies.
Nobody would like the picture of the girl,
Staring into space, a blank canvas.
Nobody would like the picture of a boy
With make-up on.
You are considered ugly
Unworthy, lonely.

We share things on social medial
Of someone trying something new
Every share is a fraction closer to suicide.
Suicide - people finally realise,
What they have done.
'Oh did you hear about the kid
Who was driven to suicide?'
But by that time they're gone.
A label - that's all it was.
It ended somebody's life.

Darcie Howard-Cahill (13)
The Albion Academy, Salford

STRONGER

Dare

I remember once when
Words used to hurt me
And just break me.

I let them get to me
I tried to break free
But what's done has been done
They went right through me.

Now, can you see?
See the new me?
Smiling and standing tall,
With my head raised high up.

Your stupid jokes and games,
Calling me nasty names.
They were so lame,
And weren't worth my pain.
Now.
I know my name!

No, I'm not on my own.
I will never be alone.
I have a mind of my own
Telling me to leave it and go.

To leave your stupid words alone.
They won't get to me. Oh no!

You don't own me;
You can't tell me what to feel.
You can't tell me what is real.
Because the happiness in me is sealed.

The hurt words are rolling away,
The good ones are coming, one day.
A new chapter,
A new day.

Rukayat Yusuff (13)
The Albion Academy, Salford

MONEY IS THE ROOT OF ALL EVIL

Truth

I cause divorces, prenups and profitable wars
Divided, added and multiplied
Interest is yours.

I wither the bones of one child
While I feed another to death
I make all the girls in the district sell what they have
And while you are stuck in those red lights
I make a path in the middle for my lovers
Whether Moscow or Mekong

Designed to be used
Not loved or misused
I'm merely an object.

I grease hands
Take lands
I decline your card, causing you a sleepless night
I party all night on a yacht in Prague
I tinge your calloused hands with desperation
As I tower a Beluga caviar on the dorsum of my hand.

Designed to be used
Not loved or misused
I'm merely an object.

If I am evil
Then doesn't that make the makers the root of all evil?

Romi Mohamed (14)
The Albion Academy, Salford

FREEDOM

Truth

All I want is freedom
To forget everything in my past
All I want is freedom
Is that too much to ask?
All I want is freedom
To clear all the pain away
All I want is freedom
To never feel that way again.

All I want is freedom
To love you my own way
All I want is freedom
To make all the tears go away
All I want is freedom
To say I love you
All I want is freedom
To hear you say, 'I love you too.'

All I want is freedom
To see everything passing by
All I want is freedom
To hear you say goodbye

All I want is freedom
To wipe the tears away
All I want is freedom
It's been so many years anyway.

Ellie Wild (13)

The Albion Academy, Salford

UNTITLED

Dare

(Inspired by 'The Hunger Games' by Suzanne Collins)

I'm trapped in a box
With no intention to survive,
I'm praying... asking God,
'Why am I still alive?'
I go to sleep knowing there is enough
For me to break down and cry.
My father taught me to be tough
And conquer my fears
My mother taught me how to love
And it's okay to shed a couple of tears.
I struggle each day to survive
Living my life with doubt.
I'm trapped in a death hole
With no hope of getting out.
I've been tormented by the devil
Ever since I was a little boy.
There is a puppet master
And I'm his number one toy.

Connor Vaughan (11)
The Albion Academy, Salford

FIRST DAY AT SCHOOL

Truth

Hesitating, I walked through the gate,
Hoping I wasn't too late.
I walked into the dining room staring at all,
As I waited to be called into the hall.
My form was with me, talking too loud,
Which made all the teachers tell us to switch down our sound.
As we were 7N, we were the last to be called in,
Which made me want to hide in a bin.
But confidently my form walked in
With the head teacher staring at us with a grin.
I sat in my seat, eagerly and proud
Of how I came in without making a sound.
I can't believe how grown up I have become,
From being a little girl who couldn't shut up.
Hopefully I stay like this
I don't want to upset Miss.

Amy Clayton (11)
The Albion Academy, Salford

MY POETIC JUSTICE

Dare

Why is it that the colour of my skin may paint an image of
hatred and violence?
Why is it that the particles in my DNA, my melanin,
may make me who I am, yet you judge me?
Why is it that the braids in my hair may symbolise poverty
and an illusion of hate?
I have brought you my gifts, my music, my culture, my food
and you have done nothing but stripped me bare and left
me as decoration used only to please those overlooking
your democracy.
I will forever be cast out by you. You do not accept me.
However I accept myself.
I have created and made you; you have left and abandoned
me.

Dieynaba Camara (14)

The Albion Academy, Salford

SCRAPBOOK

Truth

Thorns scratch my head,
Tread through that war head.
I hope to continue...
I wake up screaming.

Tortured in the night
Please!
Help me God!
Show me some sunlight.

I tried to do my best.
Constantly running away from Hell.
When I close my eyes I see the un-escaping present burning bright.
I ask myself,
Is there any sunlight?
But I know,
As long as I'm here,
There will be none of that.

I'm just a child.
Please!
I'm just a girl who needs her life.

Laiba Shafique (14)
The Albion Academy, Salford

SHADOWS

Truth

The night sky, it shadows me,
The day's shine, it reveals me,
The moon's glimmer transforms me,
The sun's brightness blinds me.

The dawn of the day fulfils me,
The dust of the night does its job and clears the streets of
the city,
The street is empty as darkness falls,
What happens next is a mystery.
It may go down in history.

Ethan Alan Walsh (11)
The Albion Academy, Salford

THE END

Truth

Ghosts everywhere haunt me,
Images of dead people watch over me,
My horrible end awaits me,
My nice memories await me.

My only friends abandon me,
People I love soon disappear,
The streets begin to riot around me,
Society has crumbled as we know it.

Everything we know has gone.

Dillon Windsor (11)
The Albion Academy, Salford

SAY NO TO GLOBAL WARMING

Dare

The Earth was on fire,
It was a dire
Situation.

Here is your warning
About global warming.
The word 'litter'
Just makes me bitter.
To kill a polar bear
Is just not fair.

Stop.
Think.
Respect.

What you are doing is killing the environment.

Luke Joseph Paul Curtis (13)
The Albion Academy, Salford

DEPRESSION

Dare

D epression is curable, those anti-depressants only help, the real cure lies within and around us, friends and family

E verything, every nerve only adds to the mental abuse they face, only true friends understand that things they do can hurt

P ut into a hole, hard to get out, left in a downward spiral, going down into a dark hole of pills and routines

R uthless, a lonely feeling that leads you to making social occasions impossible

E ndless, without the people you love and the friends you call family, people will never understand

S elfishness is all it takes to see and cause the thing that drives bonds apart

S isters and brothers may be gone but they will never be missed, you may be drowning in the insults they threw on the war ground

I nspirational, they shoot you, friends cheer you up for them only to run away as they leave you alone to be a punch bag for their words and hatred

O n the inside your mind thinks of the easy way out, but not the consequences. The knives you see, the ropes you feel make the choices easy but that is for the weak. You are strong.

N ever let the weakness get to you. Think high. If you were so bad, how did you get through it? You are strong. You are human.

Charlie Waistell (12)

Ullswater Community College, Penrith

I SHALL SHARE MY DREAMS

Truth

I trust you with my hopes and dreams,
For I am Team Truth.
Whether your name is Englebert,
Or Larry or Barry or Ruth.

My hopes and dreams are strong ones,
So I hope your mind can take it.
For I will tell the whole hard truth,
I hope that you can make it.

When I was young my dreams were seen as puny and
fragile,
Now I see the true dreams that are completely agile.
Listen closely or you'll fall away from my distant mind
And listen to the dreams to you I will bind.

My hopes and dreams are strong ones,
So I hope your mind can take it.
For I will tell the whole hard truth,
I hope that you can make it.

I have my first hope/dream right here in my grasp
So now I must destroy the everlasting clasp.

OK, I would like to become a vet
And fix up other animals, for they are other people's pets.

My hopes and dreams are strong ones,
So I hope your mind can take it.
For I will tell the whole hard truth,
I hope that you can make it.

Another of my dreams is crumbling away
So I will have to say it quickly or leave it till another day.
I would like to ride a surfboard in Australia
So if you keep on dreaming they will not fail ya'

My hopes and dreams are strong ones,
So I hope your mind can take it.
For I will tell the whole hard truth,
I hope that you can make it.

I am out of time now
So I'll leave it till another day.
Unless you see me
'round Hopeful Dream Bay.

Eleanor Harrison (11)
Ullswater Community College, Penrith

AT PEACE

Truth

A play area.
Children screaming happily like spirits of joy
The happiness spreading like fire.
The roundabout spinning like a UFO in a hurricane,
Spinning and spinning
Making you feel dizzy and sick
The swings go backwards and forwards like someone
teetering on the edge of a cliff.
A child is at peace here.

A beach.
The waves crashing against hard rocks,
Or else trickling on the soft sand.
Rock pools are dotted here and there
With hopeful eyes of children with fishing nets peering into
them,
Curious and hopeful.
Crabs scuttle here and there along the shore, pinching
people's toes.
The children play happily in the sea,
Diving and splashing and swimming and paddling,
Their parents sunbathing.
A holiday maker is at peace here.

A city.
With its bustling streets and crowded shops,
All noisy and busy,
With horns beeping and honking and blaring,
Shoppers arguing and children crying.
In the shops there are aisles and aisles of food and clothes
and other things too,
Such as cards and cardboard
There are houses and people crossing roads to soft plays.
A shopper is at peace here.

A valley.
With its many mountains and hills.
With lakes and ponds, rivers and trickling streams of crystal
waters so clear and shiny.
Little caves and crevices are dotted here and there.
Waiting for bears and other creatures to hibernate.
Pools of shining water everywhere.
I am at peace here.

Holly Saward (11)
Ullswater Community College, Penrith

HOW MY SCHOOL DAYS GO

Truth

Sometimes I feel tense and weak
But when I feel weak
I might need to shriek.
But the pain
Will always be the gain.

And when that bell goes
To tell you it's the end of the day
It will never bring the grey.

Going home
Having a cup of coffee
But without a toffee
Chilling out
But without a doubt
Watching Netflix
On electrics.

Waking up
Then getting a cup
For a morning coffee

Getting ready
But already
It's 7.50
Twenty-three minutes
Before I need to be heading for the bus.
Getting on the bus
Not many seats left
I think to myself
But I find one anyway.

Arriving at school
Knowing it's not cool
Finding my mates
There they wait
Then head to the form room
For tutor period.

Ding - the first bell goes
Reading in science
Knowing what substance
Is under the table (chewing gum).

Ding - the second bell goes
Heading to lessons
But in the right direction.
Sitting down,
Without a frown

Learning the new
Jamming it into the mind
But remembering it.

Ding - another bell goes
The bell will repeat after every lesson
Until the end of the day
And everything I just told you
Will repeat almost all the time
Except for weekend and holiday breaks
Until I leave school!

Allan Mason (11)
Ullswater Community College, Penrith

DEPRESSION

Truth

Happiness is a thing that everyone needs,
but sadness grows in your mind from seeds.
And if you don't always feel awake
and if you pretend to smile and fake
everything you do
you will never really feel like you.
But if you show your real self you won't be forgotten
so take your chance, you only have one shot
to take down the lonely roots in your mind,
to leave it all behind.
But it's not that easy, you can't fix it with a click,
it will always be there, it is something that will stick
forever, never going to leave
not a way of thinking or something you can perceive.
It's like you're trapped in a never-ending void
like all the colour, all light is destroyed.
You're just there, no great rescue or escape
It's not that you're sad, it's that you're not happy or alive;
a drowning wave which you're under trying to survive.
So it does not matter, just be you in every way
because you are who you are and that's OK.

Morgana Isobell Grave (13)
Ullswater Community College, Penrith

SNITCHES

Dare

We were the act
The one after the Spectaculars
Until we made a pact.
A pact that could protect us from the bullies
A pact that would serve us until we were dead,
We were not freaks,
Sure yeah, many of us lay awake in bed
Because we were too afraid to speak.

But yet we grew wings,
Because kids can be cruel,
Maybe we hid in the street signs
While others fought a duel.

To none of us this matters
The past is the past
Because of the battles
I'm now in a cast.

No one knows me,
People who were my friends now throw stones,
But I can always fly free,
Sticks and stones won't break my bones,
Or will they? That's yet to be seen,
The scared kid I have been.

It's time for the new kid,
It's his time to shine, his time to bid
Bid on those kids that are filled with grime
Some of those kids are going to commit crime and fight
Because of the night,
The night that whisked many away into crime.

We were the freaks,
In all different shapes and sizes,
We could never speak,
If we did we would receive prizes,
We were bullied,
And yet we were told snitches get stitches,
And those whose friends didn't listen got shoved,
But we could have spoken,
But yet snitches get stitches.

Poppy Robertson (12)
Ullswater Community College, Penrith

AGONY

Truth

I am the monster that hid in the darkness,
When you were a child,
Overactive imagination maybe,
Still left you frightened,
Still left you shivering under your covers.

When a child, barely five years old
Is told,
That the person that they loved is dead,
Who shows them why?
Who are the monsters that follow them,
Part real, part imagined
Shows them what happened.

I am the person who tells you that
You will never get anywhere,
I am the expected grade far too low,
I am the one who calls you time wasting,
Calls you a failure.

I hide in comment sections,
Computer eyes and keyboard mouths,
Tell you you are stupid,
Idiotic, pathetic.

I am those thoughts
Constant, pressing,
That tell you you are not worth it,
That everyone hates you
That you are pathetic.

I am the annoying pop songs,
Reminding you that stupid people get lucky and clever
people get nothing,
Grating into your brain,
I stay a constant annoyance.

When I am the monsters,
Parents check under the bed and say I don't exist.
But I do,
No one escapes me,
For I am the best teacher,
Yet you must never give in to me,
Never accept my opinions,
For I can be proven wrong,
And no one can ever forget that.

Skye E Wohl (13)

Ullswater Community College, Penrith

ABUSE, A SINGLE PUNCH

Dare

It's falling, the first time it fell
You couldn't recover from it.
Like diving off a cliff, into harsh, cold, muggy water
Losing your breath.
You panic, gravity brings you down,
So hard, so fast.
The stronger and lighter it is, the faster it will fall,
The heavier it is the quicker the air will get knocked straight out of you
A measly little punch.
And that single punch will happen again and again
And again you will fall.
That muggy water you fell into becomes clear, crystal water
As soon as you realise that that single punch to the gut
Was in fact called Abuse.
And abuse will come back and back,
Harder and faster than the time before.
Time is fluid,
It could drain quickly or slowly.
It could trickle down into the drain and disappear.
Then into the pipes of sadness
Then it all meets up to become one big blob of abuse.

This is about Purgatory,
The monsters and things that lurk in the dark, damp corners of Purgatory.
They unleash themselves onto passing humans
And they are the evil creators of abuse.
When they get unleashed fully,
They will become the minty chewing gum,
Sticky, grimy and disgusting on the bottom of yours and the Solar System's shoes.

Elinor Caitlin Hall (13)
Ullswater Community College, Penrith

A BLACK LAND

Dare

A black land,
No-man's-land,
Barbed wire scattered on the field,
Those hearts will never be healed.

They're never forgotten,
But they're left at the bottom,
They fade away,
While their descendents play.

Building the trenches,
Sat on the benches,
People lying dead,
It's sick in the head.

They're never forgotten,
But they're left at the bottom,
They fade away,
While their descendents play.

Explosions and gunfire,
It's still five past the hour,
Dropping bombs,
Singing songs.

They're never forgotten,
But they're left at the bottom,
They fade away,
While their descendents play.

The war fades away,
The memories stay,
Trapped in a flower
Is Britain's gratitude and power.

They're never forgotten,
But they're left at the bottom,
They fade away,
While their descendents play.

Millions of copies,
Of the same uniform poppies,
Let's celebrate,
It must be fate.

It was all done for you,
You should appreciate it too.

Jenna Davidson (12)
Ullswater Community College, Penrith

CHOOSE HOPE

Dare

All these guns and knives,
Causing endless cries,
While those devouring power,
Spend endless hours,
Building walls - not bridges
Leaving us with unclimbable ridges,
Of hate and despair - not selfless care,
For those who need it most,
So now our hearts only have a ghost,
Of long-lost brotherhood.

It's your life they say,
You can do things your way.
Yet this 'freedom of speech' comes with a price,
In some places - a life
Because you were born black
Or you were born white,
Or in the middle of a thoughtless fight
Where harmony is only a fog, just out of reach...
But let's take it back
To the fundamental fact,
We are all in this together
If we want to, or not - forever.

If our heart carries on as a minefield of hate,
It won't be long before we slam every gate
To a hope of a future
Where free people rejoice;
Instead, a land blighted by greed, a hell full of grief.
But as a whole, as this world
We all have the choice to unite,
Holding peace tight
And close to our hearts.
Silence affliction, banish war,
Unite together like never before!

Naomi Frost (13)
Ullswater Community College, Penrith

BEAUTY

Truth

No matter how much make-up I slap on
I will never be the one
No matter the designer clothes I wear
You will never care
To you I will never be perfect.
I make myself feel like I have to be beautiful
When beauty is something in your eyes I don't have
I know you will never be mine
Or take me out to wine and dine.
I need someone to be there for me
I want someone to help me be.
But you will never be that person
I just have to realise that.
To you I'm not perfect and will never be
I'm the fat friend, the ugly one
You should hang your head in shame
To you this is some sort of game.
Well I don't like playing this little game of yours
In your eyes I will never have beauty.
But, so what, I'm not your Cinderella
It's what's inside that matters, not the size of your feet.
I'm beautiful, what's it to you?
It's about me in my eyes, never about you
My life isn't a lie

Go on, I dare you, try
Try and put me down
Say I look like a clown
Stare me up and down
Make your assumption
Go on
I dare you!

Charlotte Elliott (12)
Ullswater Community College, Penrith

THE CONCRETE JUNGLE

Truth

One tree left in the city centre
It stands tall, it stands high
Once part of a jungle
Was frowned on by its own kind
Now it is surrounded by a different kind
It's now part of the concrete jungle.

This tree was once the tallest
This tree stood over all
This tree looked down on the others
This tree is no longer the tallest
This tree is smaller than all
This tree is looked down upon by the rest.

Autumn has come, leaves from the tree fall
Once was vibrant and green
Now just a dull orangy leaf on a rainy day
Now the leaves are finally falling from this one small tree
Leaves from this one small tree have fallen
They have been scattered across the city centre
They are scattered across the sky like clouds
The wind has blown them far and wide
They fall into the drains and that's where they hide.

Finally winter is over,
The sun's shining bright
This one small tree is looking green once again
It is looking vibrant and colourful
This tree is looking bushier than ever
Things are looking up for this tree.

Zoe Simpson (11)
Ullswater Community College, Penrith

HOW TO GET OVER BULLYING AND ABUSE

Dare

Never the same without him,
Gone, and gone forever,
My dad died when I was young,
He was the best, the best ever.

As if this wasn't bad enough,
My time at school was not much better,
It was cruel,
I was treated like a fool,
I hated it.

Being called fat,
And so much more,
I just wanted to hide,
And just stay there...

At home my mum hates me,
Doesn't care about me one bit,
I have no power,
I wait every second,
Every minute...
Every hour.

Everyone would be happier without me,
Nobody even cares,
I just want to go,
I can't bear it anymore.

But I knew this wasn't the way,
I started to study hard and write,
Went to college, made new friends,
Got help and wrote down all my feelings,
I changed my life...
And if you're feeling like this...
You can too.

But we need to stop bullying and abuse,
It's all getting too much,
Be kind to one another
Care and give love.

Molly Jayne Scrivens (14)
Ullswater Community College, Penrith

LET'S KEEP IT

Dare

Global warming is a pretty big thing,
Ice is melting and water is polluting.
Gas goes up and comes back down,
Snow never falls and the land is bare.
Grass never grows and flowers remain the same,
Trees come down and factories go up.
We only have one world, let's keep it.

Poverty is big and scary for some,
Living on the streets or never having fun.
Waiting and waiting nothing much to it,
When you have nothing to eat
Life is a bore,
And time seems so slow.
We only have one world, let's keep it.

Bullying is always there,
It's always in the air.
They come with abuse,
And they come with pain.
They linger in the shadows never to be seen,
When you think it's all over they come right back at you.
We only have one world, let's keep it.

War is scary, big and bold,
Can be anywhere but no one knows.
Strange things happen,
And strange things unfold.
Fighting and pain,
What good does it make?
We only have one world, let's keep it.

Rachel Huschka (13)
Ullswater Community College, Penrith

BODY IMAGE

Truth

She got up one day and looked at herself,
She needs to be concerned for her health,
A group of people called her fat yesterday,
That's why she is this way.
Her friends say she's perfect,
But that's not what she sees when the mirror reflects.
The names are stored in the back of her head,
In the morning she doesn't want to get out of bed,
She is now very skinny and fragile
All the food she hasn't eaten stacked up in a pile.
I wish someone was there to help her,
Tell her everything will be okay
But now it's happened, and things will never be the same way.
Her parents are mortified
That their little girl has lied
Telling them that she's fine
But she secretly wants to die
No matter if she was anorexic
Bulimic or mentally sick
People need to be there for each other
No matter if it's your brother, sister or another
Everyone is beautiful, no matter what,
So all this bullying has to stop.

Daisy Amber Robinson (12)

Ullswater Community College, Penrith

GOOD ENOUGH?

Truth

It's a hard thing, you know, being me.
Being happy with who I am supposed to be.
Trying not to want to interfere
With the way that I appear.
Trying not to want to change
When people call me 'stupid' or 'strange'
It's when I look in the mirror I realise
Just how much there is to criticise.
I look at myself and silently think
You'll never amount to anything.
But I go to school, I smile, I laugh,
Although I don't feel like being daft.
And every morning I manage to find,
That thing that keeps me going inside.
I think of the people who care,
Look around, they're everywhere!
They make me laugh,
They make me smile wide,
They keep me going by and by.
I can say to myself, 'I am good enough'
Even when things get tough.
I turn to the people who care
Because the people who love you are always there.

Lizzy Anne Hudspith-Spence (11)
Ullswater Community College, Penrith

ALWAYS

Truth

Each day when I wake up,
It's like I'm stuck in a repeat.
Like a clock; always punctual,
Never miss a beat.
If a single thing goes differently,
To what the normal routine would be,
Then panic will take over,
And I can begin to lose sleep.

Everything has a place,
Everything must be clean.
When I try to make this possible,
I find I'm very unique.
No one else is like this,
And no one understands.
I don't get why I'm like this,
Yet I have to stick to my plan.

My days are all the same,
However, fear always takes over.
The urge to always be clean,
Always know what is next,
Always be on time,
Always have everything in place.

It doesn't work like that,
I've found.

Each night when I go to sleep,
I am stuck in a repeat.
Everything is neat and tidy
As I begin to fall asleep.

Maisy Yates (13)
Ullswater Community College, Penrith

CHANGE

Dare

Bullies
Opinions
Hate
Love
And school...

Instead of teaching us about taxes,
It's the maths department about axis.
I mean when will we use personification
Or brackets with multiplication?
Why Henry VIII had six wives
Divorced, beheaded, died,
Divorced, beheaded, survived.

When are we even going to use French?
Or the difference between an Allen or fixed wrench
What dried yeast and hydrogen peroxide make.

But what we do need to know,
What to do if our hamstring or pectoral muscles start to ache
And if we're in debt
What to do next?
What about the effects of underage drinking
How it causes blood circulation levels to start sinking.

Not that learning that stuff doesn't matter
Just be sure you don't shatter
Under peer pressure
Make the right choices
Everything has consequences.

Alisha Chambers (13)
Ullswater Community College, Penrith

TRY ME

Truth

Happiness
The state of being happy
Abstract noun
Synonyms: joy, glee, cheerfulness
Are these really true?
Antonyms: sadness, sorrow, misery
Are these more realistic?

People's monsters can lurk in the schoolyard
Ready to leap
Ready to pounce
Others can be at home with the roaring of an argument
Over the crackling fire at the dead of night.

But most have a monster that hides upstairs,
It is up in the attic in the depths of your despair.
It taunts, it laughs, it shouts, it cries,
Willing you, telling you that you're not good enough.

Every time you think you've won,
Every time it tells you you're wrong.
It beats you like no bully could,
It torments you like nobody should
But instead of just giving up and saying, 'Why me?'
Make a change and instead say, 'Try me!'

Martha Lynam (12)
Ullswater Community College, Penrith

JUST BECAUSE I'M A LITTLE DIFFERENT...

Truth

Different? Just because I wear glasses
You think it's OK to call me 'Specky Four-Eyes'.

Just because I wear my hair different,
You think it's OK to walk past me and pull it.

Just because I have a different style of clothing to you,
You think it's OK to take the mick out of me.

Just because I have lunch by myself
You think it's OK to follow me and corner me so I can't get away...
Shout at me, laugh, call me names, beat me up
All because, because I'm a little different.

Text me saying I'm ugly, a waste of space,
I should die and I'm just a mistake...
All because I maybe like other things.

Why? What have I ever done?
What have I ever done to you?
Does it really matter, because at the end of the day
We are all human... and we all have our differences.

Zara Young (13)
Ullswater Community College, Penrith

ME!

Dare

Hey, see I am writing this rap
Cos there is always something behind my back.
I have some feelings I need to share
But I need someone to actually care.
Nobody cares.
I need to see what is actually happening,
The depression is rising there is no happiness
And then I found someone
But then he was gone.
Yes, he is gone, see my life is never perfect
I thought I wasn't worth it
Then I saw that people understood me
But then they betrayed me behind my back
I thought I was worth much more than that.
That's when the trust issues came out
Is that all I am about?
To be treated like a tool
Now I feel like a fool.
My life was never perfect
Then I remember that I am worth it
All those feelings inside
I have nothing to hide.
It's made me realise I am me
And it's who I want to be.

Poppy Carr (11)

Ullswater Community College, Penrith

EDUCATION

Dare

Sometimes I wonder if there's any need for education,
Did it happen by choice or accident?
Too often we lose our mind finding the answers
An answer or solution isn't at the back of a maths text book.
The answer is in your mind,
Don't forget your book and pencil case.
How many times do we tell you to bring your equipment?
How could teachers have the standardisation to create tests?
A pen and paper isn't going to prepare you for life's quests.
Time to think about the situation in the real world.
To teach is to tell stories and help with maths and English,
We want education to help us in life,
Sometimes we feel like we're not good enough for school.
Sometimes we need a challenge,
When we find out that we've got A* and A,
We say, 'Thank you for school and education.'

Aimee Fowles (13)
Ullswater Community College, Penrith

STILL

Dare

Still this day
Family members are dying
Animals disappear
Children are crying
Then reappear...
But not as themselves.

Still this hour
Crash! another tree gone
Bang! another car made
Swoosh! no more birds singing their songs
Do we really need to make our planet fade?

Still this minute
People are plotting
Fighting all day
As the bodies are rotting
They slowly fade away.

Still this second
I'm reading this poem
Trying to win you over
As people still bully Owen
And what for?
He's not a four-leafed clover.

Sticks and stones
May break our bones
But no one can stop emotion
We stand together!
Not alone.
Speak out!

Maddison Elliott (12)
Ullswater Community College, Penrith

DARING TO BE DIFFERENT

Dare

Humanity is crumbling,
Society is declining
Our lives are filled with constant chaos,
We forget what really matters.

We fight fire with fire,
Violence with violence
We hurt others
We discriminate differences.

So what if a girl likes a girl?
If someone isn't comfortable in their own skin
It is disgusting how the community acts,
Like animals and not human.

Equality has been forgotten;
They are human just like you!
With war and poverty around us
Yet we focus on people's differences.

The world has bigger problems,
Than boys that kiss boys
And girls that kiss girls

Our sexuality doesn't define us,
Neither should it define you.

Anna Victoria Hogg (12)
Ullswater Community College, Penrith

DEAR GRANDAD

Truth

Now the sky has another star,
I will see it and know that you're not far
As life goes on, I know,
That you have been there to watch me grow.

You were the funniest grandad ever, simply the best!
A loving, caring man, a cut above the rest.
And even though I miss you, I know,
That you were an Armstrong and would never let pain show.

You have taught me so much and I will never forget,
Times with you shepherding, getting muddy and wet.
Feeling privileged to be with you at Longtown auction mart,
Helping in the ring and really feeling the part.

I knew you were there, and how much you cared,
And I will always remember the memories we shared.

Lots of love Olivia xx

Olivia Armstrong (12)
Ullswater Community College, Penrith

DANCE IS FOR LIFE

Dare

Dance is for life.
I have been doing it since I was little
In fact since I could walk.
Truly, dance is for life.
It is not just dance that makes me happy,
Singing, dancing, playing, doing everything that I love to do.
The reason I am telling you this
Is because life is hard, really hard.
I have been through something
That millions of children go through every day
So this is what I want to say
Do something you love and do it for life.
So you have something that you love.
That's when the world changes and you change
You have something that is the same
But that does not mean that you should not step out of your comfort zone
Go for it, love life
But do something for life.

Nicole Wallace (12)
Ullswater Community College, Penrith

DRUGS

Dare

Drugs, drugs
Think of the cost,
Of your life once it's been lost.
You cannot get it back,
You need no crack.

Your life will turn dark
And leave a big mark,
Drugs are bad
It won't make you a lad.

Your mates do it
Don't take a hit
It's bad for you
It will leave a clue
You'll be locked up.

Drugs are bad,
They'll make you mad
Don't go crazy
It will leave you hazy.

Weed, weed,
Isn't something you need,
Weed can kill,
It will leave you with a bill.

You may think it's cool,
But you are the fool,
Weed's a bad thing,
It doesn't make you king.

Luke Coulston (13)
Ullswater Community College, Penrith

STOP TERRORISM!

Dare

Stop!
All this crime and war is unacceptable,
You're ruining homes, lives and people,
This world is not about war,
Some people can't describe what they saw.
You're decreasing population,
So get on the next train at the station.
When terrorists attack, they are just like a wolf pack,
When terrorists get shot, it ruins their evil plot.
Every bullet you fire,
And every bomb you drop,
It makes you think you're at the top,
But they know one day they will flop.

I'm just fighting for what I believe in,
So don't be deceiving.
So stop or the world will end,
Because we have something worth living for,
Spend more time with your friends.

Alex (12) & Danny Lund (12)
Ullswater Community College, Penrith

MY BULLYING STORY

Dare

I strutted into the room announcing my team,
That's when the bullying really started to kick in.
It made me feel uncomfortable, it made me feel alone,
When the babbling arose from a room unknown.
Bullying is nice, you should try it,
Huh! I'm joking. You really think I mean that?
Say I look like a tramp, that's not encouraging,
That's because I've just been beaten up by the bullies.
I'm meant to be fighting
I know there's a rule against hate crime
Just wondering, do you like my rhyme?
That's the end for the time being
I hope you understood what I was saying
It's not a game, no one is playing
No bullying!

Alice Rose Wade (11)
Ullswater Community College, Penrith

BULLYING FLAWS

Dare

Kids are cruel
They only bully you
Because you are at school.
It doesn't matter what your race is,
It doesn't matter what they say
Doesn't matter about your background
Don't let them hurt your face.
They might not like you
But you shouldn't care,
So just say
Beware, beware of things you do to me
You life is empty
Go sit in a tree.
You're gonna get caught
They are always there
Trying to watch you
Trying to hurt.
Looking at your body
Counting the flaws
Do not be afraid
Just slam the door.

Go in a bin
Look at yourself
You're not a sin
You need some help.

Danny Beaty (12)
Ullswater Community College, Penrith

CONSEQUENCES

Truth

'You have no friends!'
'You are ugly and stupid!'
Their insults are constantly there.
Like a woodpecker, pecking at their brain.
They tell you lies that seem too real to believe.
The user doesn't understand how serious it can be,
Taking people's friends and life.
Too scared to speak out,
Too scared to make new friends
Or even tell their parents.
Cyber bullying is a life-changing event,
It can change someone forever.

Have you understood what you've done?
Do you realise how you've made them feel?
A thousand tears have been shared
A part of their life that can never be repaired.

Jasmine Keisha Bellas (11)
Ullswater Community College, Penrith

TERRORISM

Dare

I am Dare,
My role is to make you push yourself to the limit
Time to face terrorism.

I float around listening to conversations
All include terrorism
People need to face their fears
And stand up for themselves
Hey, you there, have you ever stood up for yourself?
Go on tell me!
Of course you haven't
We need to stand together against terrorism.

Some people who are capable of fighting don't
They just hide away, hoping it will end
But it won't, it's getting closer as we speak.
People need to come out of their shells
They could be heroes.
In fact I dare you to help fight terrorism.

Liam Ludgate (11)
Ullswater Community College, Penrith

TRUTH OR DARE

Truth

Will you choose both truth or dare?
I don't know, they are a pair.
I think I will choose the truth,
Like I'm in a photo booth.

Maybe like my biggest secret,
I really hope you can keep it.
Maybe like I suck my thumb,
I didn't want to tell anyone.

Or like my biggest fear,
A big spider will make a tear.
So that is my poem for truth or dare,
That I put in a lot of care.

You will have a good competition,
It will be a great mission.
I can't really rhyme any longer,
So good luck and goodbye
If you choose the truth side,
Please oh please do not lie.

Emily Chambers (11)
Ullswater Community College, Penrith

UNKNOWN PERSON

Dare

There was a stranger there
Standing in the middle of the road.
Silently playing with their hair
Oblivious to their certain death.

She was clearly quite upset
Standing in the middle of the road
Everyone had tasks and jobs to do
Time stopped in its tracks.

Everything for just one second was silent
Standing in the middle of the road
Then everything went red and the scene turned violent
The sound of car tyres screeching and terrified screams.

Life shouldn't be like this ever
Standing still through life
Why should things be like this?
Enjoy life while you can...

Callum Popple (13)
Ullswater Community College, Penrith

FEELINGS ARE DANGEROUS

Truth

Feelings are dangerous
Why do we feel the need to bring people down?
You're ugly,
You're dumb,
You're weird,
You're not normal and don't belong here.

It is hard enough to face the world,
Without the people in it making it harder,
A simple word or compliment
It doesn't cost at all,
It could put a person's self-esteem as high as the moon.

Don't be scared to stand up for yourself,
The world is what you make it,
Big or small it's yours to decide.
But make it worth it,
Your time on Earth is short and sweet,
So live it to the full.

Ellie Miller (13)
Ullswater Community College, Penrith

SOCIAL MEDIA

Dare

S napchat is for sharing things with your friends

O f course this is ace but people also stalk

C ommunicating with your friends immediately and more

I nappropriate pictures being sent all over the country

A buse is happening and people wanting money

L ikewise with YouTube creativity happens every day

M inds that think alike all over the world

E ndless contacting all day every day

D epression is happening

I know lots is good but there are people's minds being messed with every day

A mazingly, there are good things in every way.

Millie Emma Bainbridge (11)

Ullswater Community College, Penrith

ANIMALS

Dare

Animals are so nice and hardly make a mistake
So why do we cook them and turn them into steak?
Why do we eat animals most of the time?
Can we not just have a lemon and lime?

Animals are so, so nice to us,
Don't they at least deserve to go on a bus?
Can we please stop eating them?
Animals are so nice, I prefer them to a gem.

I really want you and I to stop all this
I know there are some animals we don't like
Like the ones that hiss.
Don't they deserve to have names like Joe or Tom?
Those are proper names
And this is the poem that will win The Poetry Games.

Joe Mortimer (11)
Ullswater Community College, Penrith

CONTROLLED

Truth

When you're being controlled
You don't see it.

You think they love you
They just want something of you
When they have what they want they leave
This isn't anything but humans
But why? Why do this?
They think they're big, strong, the boss
They're really not, they're just controlling you
People try to tell you
But you're blinded by the person
When you try to leave
They won't let you
They might abuse you
We need to stop this
It could be you next
Just stay away from those people
Before you know it you'll have no money.

Jack Graham (13)
Ullswater Community College, Penrith

DONALD

Dare

I know you don't believe in global warming,
In the streets protesters are storming.
No one likes the travel ban,
All you've got is an orange tan.

It's not all silly though, it's serious too
Sexism, racism all coming from you.
Not letting transgender people join the army
You're making the whole country go barmy.

With World War Three around the corner,
Donald Trump get out of your sauna.
Guns and knives are bad,
Look what happened in Las Vegas, that was sad.

You think guns are good,
People stop using them with a thud.

Arran Robert Gilpin (12)
Ullswater Community College, Penrith

EVERYONE IS DIFFERENT

Dare

Everyone is different,
No one is the same.
So why when someone is different
Do they feel the pain?

When someone stands out
Wears different clothes
Or has a different phone
Why do they loathe?

Everyone is different,
No one is the same.
So why when someone is gay
Should they feel lame?

If someone is different
Why should it matter.
If you're being mean
It will make their lives shatter.

Everyone is different,
No one is the same.
People shouldn't be mean
It isn't a game.

Lillie Dixon (13)
Ullswater Community College, Penrith

ABOUT ME

Truth

So I'm telling you the truth, a secret and maybe some more,
A little few secrets, I hope you don't tell.
So I'm sorry if this poem starts to bore,
I may shout a little but I'm trying not to yell!

So a bit about me, I'm blonde, blue eyes and as happy as can be,
I don't have glasses, nor braces, if you can see.
I like music, pop's the best
I always show up nicely dressed!

I'm an auntie to a five-year-old boy,
My sister owns a lot of toys.
Hair and beauty is my absolute way
Bye for now, that's all I'm gonna say...

Ella Harrison (11)
Ullswater Community College, Penrith

GIRL POWER

Dare

G irls are not stupid, they're bright

I f boys think otherwise they will get a fright

R ight to vote, that's what women declared

L ife isn't always simple, it can be a dare.

P owder, lipstick and eyeshadow is part of a girl's confident life

O n the other hand boys must understand this if they want a wife

W omen are allowed to express themselves and have their voices heard

E ven when boys refer to them as being their 'bird'

R ight, come on girls, let's not cower, let's use our Girl Power!

Erin Sowerby (13)

Ullswater Community College, Penrith

IN A MINUTE

Truth

The years have passed by
People I loved have come and gone
But the world never stopped
We just carried on.

And the worries and fears
That plagued me each day,
In the end of it all
Would just fade away.

But how much I reached out
To others when needed
Would be the true measure
Of how I succeeded.

And what's really important
Is my opinion of me
And whether or not
I'm the best I can be.

And how much kindness
And love I can show
Before the Lord tells me
It's my time to go.

Ellie Chan (13)
Ullswater Community College, Penrith

GROWING UP

Truth

Growing up is an adventure,
Growing up is exploring the world,
Growing up is a chance,
Your chance to have fun!

Exploring vast lands,
Miles of countryside,
Seeing the sea,
Exploring immense cities,
Seeing the wonders of the world.

You can watch fireworks go bang,
Rushing waterfalls,
Dripping raindrops,
Slurping mud beneath your boots.

You can watch roaring skies,
Confused clouds,
Winking stars at night.

You can be anyone,
Anything,
Go anywhere,
See everything...

Tom Nicholson (12)
Ullswater Community College, Penrith

RACIAL INEQUALITY

Dare

In Africa it started,
When people's rights parted,
People were forbidden,
Restricted like a child.

In some places they're not accepted,
In others they're discriminated,
They want to be as free as a bird,
But they can't after the news they heard.

It's illegal in some countries,
But still goes on in others.
Some people are banned from places,
Because of their colour.

People try to make it fair,
And fight against racism.
They just want to make it equal,
And combine the schism.

Joshua Yerkess (11)
Ullswater Community College, Penrith

THE PREDATOR

Dare

Lurking slyly behind your screen
Ruthless predators prowl.
Like a fox hunting savagely
On a dark and lonely night.

Predators are arrows waiting
For the time to strike
You are their helpless target
Knowing something isn't right.

All seeming too real
Like a hand is creeping through
The screen then throttling you by the neck
Until you start to scream.

Finally your phone alerts you
Firstly with texts and threats
Then silence sweeps across your room
Followed by three eerie knocks...

Hannah Louise Holmes (11)
Ullswater Community College, Penrith

NERVES BEFORE THE FINAL

Dare

The blood projecting through my head,
The panic for the big final.
My hair's on end,
My legs tremble to the end
The leathery smell of the leather ball,
It's taunting me.
The boot connecting to the grass,
Sounds like metal on metal.
The crowd are staring like mad,
And my palms are sweating like mad,
With all the nerves in my head
I can't hear the coach
The crowd shout 'United!'
It sounds like a crowd of Indians shooting
We do the handshakes
I am reflecting as we're waiting
Then the whistle blew.

Willan Jim Wallace (11)
Ullswater Community College, Penrith

WHY OH WHY?

Dare

Why oh why?
This question travels internationally
Why do people have to bully?
Why have they to be so mean?
Why do they have to bring you down?

Why oh why?
They can do it face to face,
Or even online,
Why can't they just not do it at all?

Why oh why?
They call you names
And hurt your feelings
Laugh about you behind your back

The only thing I'm trying to get across is...

Why oh why
Can't all this stop.
Why oh why
Do they have to do this?

Lottie Sharratt (12)
Ullswater Community College, Penrith

THE CREATURES

Dare

Whales are dead
The oil has been spread
Sea creatures dying
The humans denying.

The ocean is polluted
It's really not suited
No more fish
For our dish.

Beautiful creatures in danger every day
It doesn't have to be this way
Oil, nets, boats
I can tell you now, polluting the sea will get no votes.

We have to treat the animals in this world like treasure
Let them swim at their leisure.
No killing, no suffering and no evil
We all need to be happy like a pop-up weasel.

Isabel Sanderson (12)
Ullswater Community College, Penrith

TRUTH OR DARE!

Dare

'Truth or dare Peter?'
'Dare!'
'I dare you to push that little girl over!'
'Okay!'

'Zara, how did it make you feel
When he did that?'
'It hurt and I think Peter is evil!'

'Truth or Dare, Peter?'
'Dare!'
'I dare you to push that little girl over!'
'No!'

'Zara, how did that make you feel?'
'I am so glad
That Peter did not push me over!'

'Which Peter would you be?'

Jack Wallace (11)
Ullswater Community College, Penrith

CHOOSING

Dare

Only thirteen and fourteen years old!
People telling you that you need to decide now,
Options coming really quick,
People telling you what you should do,
'Do this, you would be good at it.'

Not knowing what to choose,
People asking,
'What are you choosing?'
Teachers telling you why to do that subject,
So much pressure!

In the end you have to choose,
Thinking of your future,
So young and undecided,
Stressing and wondering what to do,
Thinking *what do I do?*

Annabel Murphy (14)
Ullswater Community College, Penrith

THE NATURE'S TRUTH

Truth

Have you heard of nature?
It is a lovely thing,
Mountains, animals, trees,
Nature is what they are.

The trees protect us with the air,
And I protect my dogs with my heart,
The animals keep their promise to the circle of life,
As it's their role,
The mountains protect animals like a lifeguard at sea.

I am telling the truth here,
Why would I not?
The world is as beautiful as a rainbow and better,
Come on out and look around,
Nature is your garden,
It's just waiting for you!

Samantha Anne Bufton (11)
Ullswater Community College, Penrith

CHOICE

Dare

Don't let anyone tell you what to do,
Or how to do it,
It's your choice!
When people don't believe in you,
Make them believe in you,
It's your choice!
Don't let anyone boss you around
'Cause you know yourself better than anyone else does,
It's your choice.
And you know how to live your life
Don't let anyone else tell you how to live it,
It's your choice
Follow your heart, believe in yourself
And don't let anyone tell you how to do it,
It's your choice.

Honey Railton (11)
Ullswater Community College, Penrith

OUR HEROES

Dare

This needs to change,
People get millions for kicking a ball around,
And they risk their lives for a couple of pounds,
They're not forgotten
One injury and you're at rock bottom.
So much just to get fit,
Running around with all the heavy kit,
And what do they get back from this?
Nothing.

Now onto another,
Risk it all just for the mothers
But don't forget the father
They're the reason you work harder,
We should all aspire to be them
They are all our heroes!

Rhys Connor Akrigg (12)
Ullswater Community College, Penrith

THE HARD LIFE OF ANIMALS

Truth

On the outside, I feel small,
On the inside, I feel tall,
I am as small as a pin,
But my heart is as big as a metal tin,
Being an animal is hard.

I am as proud as a king,
But my kindness is as small as a ring,
I wish I was as thoughtful as the others,
Who were taught to share by their mothers,
Being an animal is hard.

I am as fast as light,
But I have lost my might.
I used to be as strong as a bear,
But now I am as weak as a pear.
Being an animal is hard.

Esmé Millie Fawcett (11)
Ullswater Community College, Penrith

BEHIND CLOSED DOORS

Dare

One happy street,
With many happy faces,
But one door is different,
The owners never surfacing,
And the muffled shouts and yells echo through the walls,
But only at night-time,
When they think we can't hear,
But we can.

And the panelled door blocks us out,
And the window blinds pulled down,
Shielding a secret,
One you can't deny,
So when the child walks to school,
Having been beaten,
Hiding his bruise,
He says he's fine,
But he's not.

Heather Mein (13)
Ullswater Community College, Penrith

MY MESSAGE TO YOU

Truth

Feeling like a bird up in the sky,
I know I'm being bullied, this isn't a lie.
My emotions have come just to say hi,
But they will never say bye, bye, bye.

I'm feeling warm, cold, worried and scared
I don't know what to do
What should I do?
Why did they do it?
Who should I tell?

Bullies are careful, sneaky and devious,
My message to you,
Is to stand up tall
And don't let the bullies bother you at all.

Jessie Ridley (11)
Ullswater Community College, Penrith

FRIENDSHIP

Dare

You are my best friend, you belong in my heart,
We go through ups and downs but nothing can keep us
apart.
I know you as a sister, I will always care,
Love, respect and trust are the three things we share.

I know you as a person and a friend,
Our friendship is something that will never end.
Right this second, this minute, this day,
Our sisterhood is here, here to stay.
My friendship with you is very true,
When we are together, we stick like glue.

Natasha Jade Malloy (11)
Ullswater Community College, Penrith

THE TRUTH IS OUT!

Truth

Finally, the truth is out!
Have you ever met,
Or will meet,
A monster
It was once a human,
With a nice, pleasant, kind,
Genuine and loving heart.
It is as soft as silk.

A jealous, spiteful person,
Came out,
And stole the loving heart,
And turned them into the same as them!

Next time when you see,
A monster,
Do not panic,
Or create a scene,
Because they will,
Come back
And haunt you.

D'arcy Bell (12)
Ullswater Community College, Penrith

DEMENTIA

Truth

I go to see him, he doesn't remember me,
Not even my name.
He can barely remember what he has eaten
Never mind me.

The only thing he remembers is the World War
Every single detail
He is dying now
And I don't want to go visit him in hospital.

I wish I could go back to when he remembered
And he gave me a KitKat every time we saw him
But he has dementia now
And they don't know how long he will live.

Joe Braithwaite (13)
Ullswater Community College, Penrith

MY PARENTS

Truth

Even though my parents are divorced
Mum doesn't make me feel forced,
Just 'cause they've split up
It doesn't mean they've given up.
Mum tells me 'You never frown
You never ever let us down.'
They inspire me constantly
To be the best that I can be.
If you know how I feel
I'm sure you can agree
Even the worst hasn't brought them down
They definitely deserve cuddly nights in their dressing
gowns.

Jack Wilson (11)
Ullswater Community College, Penrith

DIFFERENT

Truth

D ifferent does not mean you don't fit in

I ndividuality separates people

F orever and always being you

F orever and always being me

E ven if people say I'm weird of different

R ise up before them and show them who's boss

E ventually everyone will realise...

N obody is the same as each other

T ime to tell and show everyone that I am different in some type of way.

Rianna Harrison (11)

Ullswater Community College, Penrith

GONE

Dare

Along the beach everything falls
Along the beach we feel so small
As everything scattered everything lies
Everything is gone.

Butterflies go by
Horses run along
Dogs chasing sheep
Everything all gone.

Fish in the sea
Birds in the sky
Mammals on land
Now just humans conquering the land.

As I walk there is no more
As I walk I hear a thunderous roar.

Danny Eland (11)
Ullswater Community College, Penrith

WAR

Dare

For years people have
Fought in great wars
But the truth is all they've
Been fighting for is
Nothing.

Absolutely nothing
It's just land, soil, water.
If you looked at it now
It's just angry people.
Don't get angry.

You only get one shot at life
Don't waste it fighting for
Something that will probably
Get taken from you the
Next year.

Reece Teasdale (11)
Ullswater Community College, Penrith

THE TRUTH ABOUT ME

Truth

I am a sporty person
Who plays a lot of football,
Apart from in the summer
As I play a lot of cricket.

When I play football
I really feel competitive.
Even if I win or if I lose,
My team don't say any boos.

When I play cricket I like to win,
But when we lose I don't like to show any sign
I just keep my feelings inside
I like sports, I am competitive.

Tegan Mai Parkin (11)
Ullswater Community College, Penrith

MY LIFE

Truth

My life is so cool, I have my own tools.
I have a nice house, and a great couch.
My mum's a great cook, and has lots of luck.
I have a nice bed, where I lay my head.
I have nice clothes and cute toes.
I have great toys that make lots of noise.
I have a nice garden, oops, pardon.
I play on a trampoline with my team.
I go to the barn near the farm.
I have a good time making a rhyme!

Alfie Hay (11)
Ullswater Community College, Penrith

FIGHTING FOR THE WORLD

Truth

The horrible battlefield full of blood and a lot of mud.
It may be scary but we must fight for what is ours.
Some may be cowards, some may be heroes
But if we fight hard we could take back our country with a full-on gun attack.
We need to win this for the people of the world,
We'll keep this place safe so our future will be real.
They may steal our land but they will never take away our country.

Elliot Baty (11)
Ullswater Community College, Penrith

CREATION

Truth

C ome with me and you will see

R ainforests and all things big and small

E ach thing in the world is special

A nd you and me need to value the world

T ogether we will celebrate the world

I n different parts and places

O ther people in the world need to admire this wonderful world

N ow we need to show how great this world really is.

Molly-Jane Guy-Gregg (11)

Ullswater Community College, Penrith

WORLD OF WAR

Truth

War is happening all the time,
For selfish people are attacking.
Lovely people are losing the people they love,
Going to Heaven up above.
Attackers who think they are in control
Soldiers trying to help the community, risking their lives
It affects the world in so many ways, people are terrified.
I wish it would stop
The world is tearing apart,
Making so many problems.

Rachel Abbott (11)
Ullswater Community College, Penrith

UNENDING

Dare

Neglected, rejected
Too quiet, too hush.

Being friendless feels endless
Everyone seems in a rush.

I'm just a kid,
But I want rid
No one will ever see me as rad.

Sympathy, pity,
It's stupid, it's silly

I'll never fly
So I might as well die.

I guess I'll see you another time.

Ella Philips (11)
Ullswater Community College, Penrith

UNTITLED

Dare

On top of a mountain,
Or underwater
There are a lot of places
Where animals and creatures can be.

Alone in cages
Or in a desert
Or in some trees
Some in harm, some not.

In bright sunny places,
In freezing and icy Arctic
Jungles and forests
There are so many places animals and creatures are
But some are not treated nicely.

Charlie Southworth (12)
Ullswater Community College, Penrith

PEOPLE

Dare

People are big or small,
Some are young and others are old,
It doesn't matter the colour of your skin,
Some speak different languages,
Age doesn't matter, it's what you do,
We have disabilities but we still live life like a normal person,
We're not stupid because of dyslexia,
We are as smart as everyone else,
People are the best thing in life.

Jack Bowman (11)
Ullswater Community College, Penrith

MY SWEET FOREVER CAT

Truth

Your eyes are blue
Your fur is soft
Your ears prickle against the frost
Up in the clouds
You will see
That forever is for you and me
My sweet forever cat.

Your purr so sweet
Your curly tail
The things you did
When you were here
I know right now
Because you are not here
There's something missing
My sweet forever cat.

Jessica Brown (12)
Ullswater Community College, Penrith

DRUGS

Dare

It's not really smart
You'll live alone in the dark
Unable to pay for what you need
Because you spend all your money on weed
Now I'm not joking
You should really stop smoking
But you can't because you're addicted
And you couldn't have predicted
This could be your life
Get a grip and sort it out
Do it without a doubt.

Josh Padgett (13)
Ullswater Community College, Penrith

SCHOOL RULES

Truth

I think school times should be lowered,
Especially in the morning when we are tired.
I think we should have breaks between every lesson,
So that our minds are bright and ready.
I think we should be allowed our phones at break,
So we can call our mums and tell them how our day is.
I think we should be allowed to choose our lessons
So we can pursue what we want to.

Cody Robert Jackson (11)
Ullswater Community College, Penrith

TRUTH

Truth

Truth is about believing,
Truth is about being you
Truth is a never-ending experience
Truth can lead you through.

Truth is your ambitions,
Your hope,
Your eternity,
Whatever it is you can show it
With the power of truth.

Whatever it may be, share it
Tell people about your ambitions
It will happen with the truth.

Emily Mawson (11)
Ullswater Community College, Penrith

DOGS

Truth

Music in my ears
Cute, fluffy dogs,
Out in the sun
They play every day
Whenever I say.

My heart is broken
My life is gone
I have nowhere to go
Except to my mum.

Me and my mum spending our time
At home playing board games
When my dad comes back home he goes to bed
He sleeps all day and then goes to work.

Matti Kowal (12)
Ullswater Community College, Penrith

EDUCATION

Truth

E very child needs to be educated

D o your best

U nderstand the value of learning

C an you learn? Of course you can!

A lways enjoy learning new things

T o be amazing you must practise

I magination is the key

O nly you can do it

N ow it is time for you to try your best to achieve what you want.

Dominic Horrobin (12)

Ullswater Community College, Penrith

EMPTY LIFE

Dare

I'm just a hole,
In your soulless empty life.
I'm just like a mole,
Searching for daylight.

You pull me in,
Then push me out.
I feel like a bin
Without a doubt.

I feel hurt
As if I'm dead
You put me in
My forever bed.

I'm just a hole,
In your soulless empty life.

Ryan Carrick (13)
Ullswater Community College, Penrith

TRUTH

Truth

In life you don't need to lie,
Just tell the truth and you'll be fine.
No need to be a tell-tale,
Still doesn't mean you're gonna fail.
Tell the truth,
Sometimes you don't want to get into trouble,
Doesn't mean you have to lie,
Lying can be bad at times,
So just tell the
Truth!

Morgan Goad (11)
Ullswater Community College, Penrith

STEALING

Dare

Stealing is foolish,
If only we had a way to stop it all
You never know, time will show
Stealing leads to violence
Violence leads to wars
Wars lead to devastation
You will then realise
Out of all the people dying
Out of all the people enslaved
And the starving people;
You started it all.

Dominic Blenkharn (11)
Ullswater Community College, Penrith

POP! BANG! BOOM!

Truth

Pop! Bang! Boom!
The fireworks go *boom!*
Rockets dancing in the jet-black sky,
Gathering sticks so the bonfire doesn't die,
Sizzling sausages and fizzy Coke,
People coughing in a cloud of smoke,
Remember, remember the 5th November,
Getting colder as it's almost December.

Melissa Clark (11)
Ullswater Community College, Penrith

EDUCATION

Dare

School
School all comes down to a test
A test that makes your life career
Apparently
A letter on a page
Life shouldn't all come to one test
So if your job is good or bad
It's not always that
Remember life careers aren't
Being made by a letter on a page.

Sam Bayliffe (13)
Ullswater Community College, Penrith

DARE TO BE TRUE

Dare

As deep as the sea is blue
As yellow as the sun shines bright
I dare you to have the courage of a lion
I dare you to keep your dreams alive,
To follow your heart until the end.
For this is the true beauty inside the Earth
And this is the strength within us all,
All we have to do is believe!

Ella Hall (11)
Ullswater Community College, Penrith

IT WAS TIME...

Dare

The bullying began
And I was all alone
I met someone new
They told me, 'Be you!'
I started to think
And took their advice
I realised it was time
And put them right.
They'll never admit it
But I swear it's true
I hope this never happens again to me or you!

Kira McDonald (11)

Ullswater Community College, Penrith

FREEDOM

Dare

F ree, the birds fly high in the dark sky

R ide nice and high where the butterflies fly

E ventually with all these bad lies

E qually divided with my hair ties

D reams demolished by high skies

O pportunities tried

M ove with blessed endings.

Keeley Thompson (14)

Ullswater Community College, Penrith

BEST FRIENDS

Truth

You are my pride and joy
We are always together.
There is no way we are inseparable
We do everything as two.
You stick with me through thick and thin
I am never alone
When you are by my side
I love you with all my heart
Stay with me always!

Tia Holly Emmens (13)
Ullswater Community College, Penrith

OUR WAY OF LIFE

Dare

We chop the trees without care
Without knowing what's lurking there
Like a tear
So think before you drink
Or maybe think before you blink
Think of the suffering
The pain the animals go through
So if I were you
I'd think...

Katie Jade White (11)
Ullswater Community College, Penrith

UNTITLED

Truth

My loving, loyal friend
He's two years old,
His colour is salt and pepper,
And his nature very bold.

He wakes me up in the morning,
Excited for his treat,
He's very protective of us all,
This dog would be hard to beat.

Erin Dixon (11)
Ullswater Community College, Penrith

BEING DIFFERENT

Dare

Being different isn't bad,
You stand out from the crowd
Be who you are and what you want to be,
You can speak aloud.

Don't be afraid to show the real you
Because you are you, be proud and true.

Lily Anne Kitching (14)
Ullswater Community College, Penrith

EVEN TIME

Dare

Humans are like space,
When disaster strikes,
Humans are like apes,
With fingers and thumbs.

All comes to an end,
Everything and everyone,
Things take their demise,
Even time... and space.

James Heape (11)
Ullswater Community College, Penrith

TERRORISM

Dare

Innocent people dying,
Innocent children crying
Bombs exploding, guns firing,
Will this ever end?

Why do they do it?
What is the point?
Will someone stop them?
Will this ever end?

Aidan Powell-Currie (11)
Ullswater Community College, Penrith

AFTERMATH

Truth

The bombs have been dropped
The soldiers are dead
All of this stuff can't fit in my head
Everything is gone
And there is nothing we can do
We are left with a wasteland
And everything is dead.

Daniel Harrison (13)
Ullswater Community College, Penrith

FREEDOM

Dare

F ree to do what I want to do

R ights have been won

E at when I want to

E verlasting fun.

D o what I want

O ppression will stop

M y life is mine again.

Robbie Forsyth (13)
Ullswater Community College, Penrith

RACISM

Dare

The world should not be divided
The world should be united
Petty differences
We should not be separated because of the colour of our skin
Or the religion we believe
We should be united.

Kieran Eland (13)
Ullswater Community College, Penrith

THE TRUTH

Truth

Animals are good, not bad
So it does not mean we can kill just to be glad
Animals never hurt you so why do you
Animals need to be free
Not locked up in a cage to see
It is not fair, so stop!

Libby Burne (11)
Ullswater Community College, Penrith

TERRORISM

Dare

For one last time, stop terrorism
From Manchester to New York
Stop terrorism.

What is meant,
Is just makes a dent
They say God told them to do it,
But he didn't.

Morgan Bland (11)
Ullswater Community College, Penrith

FREEDOM

Truth

Mason is my name,
I don't want to be the same,
I definitely don't want the fame,
I just want to be free,
As free as a bird in the sky,
Flying up, higher than high.

Mason McAneney (12)
Ullswater Community College, Penrith

YOUNG CARERS

Dare

Y ou may think I am just a person who looks after their mum, dad and loved ones but no, I put the hope in hopeful and I put the happy in happiness

O ur community needs support in the young carers make believe to make others aware of what we are going through

U nderstand what we are going through and support us if we need it

N ow stand next to me when I need a shoulder to cry on, a hand to hold and someone to love and care for me even at the saddest of times

G uide me through life and when the times get hard help me.

C o-operate if I am struggling with work, help me

A id me when I need assistance

R ely on me if you have any secrets I will keep them safe

E njoy being friends with me and cherish every moment

R espect us, we deserve to be treated like any other person.

Remember young carers are like any other person
Think before you act, don't bully us
Because you don't know what is going on at home.

Safia Schulz (11)
Weatherhead High School, Wallasey

IF YOU SHALL DARE...

Dare

Try to tell me,
If you shall dare,
One little lie,
And one little truth.

Your foolishness is full of lies,
Now tell me,
It's survive or die,
Your time is running out.

Look at me,
From eye to eye,
Your posture shows that you're jealous,
Now is the time.
Tick, tick, tick.

Your luck is now over,
You shall hide under your duvet,
However not for very long,
As I shall find you.

Now run...

Ellie Frost (12)
Weatherhead High School, Wallasey

LOVE NEEDS PATIENCE

Truth

Love is really hard to find,
If you want love go and hide,
It may not be easy but soon it will come,
When you treasure them, they'll have some fun.
They may be grateful, they may not be kind
But deep down really they love you inside.
They may kiss you, they may hug you,
They may write to you too
But true love isn't either, texting to you.
They write you cheesy paras, they cheat on people too,
So what's even the point in doing anything new?

Hope Susan Lucas (12)
Weatherhead High School, Wallasey

YOUNG WRITERS
INFORMATION

We hope you have enjoyed reading this book – and
that you will continue to in the coming years.

If you're a young writer who enjoys reading and creative
writing, or the parent of an enthusiastic poet or story writer,
do visit our website **www.youngwriters.co.uk**. Here you will
find free competitions, workshops and games, as well as
recommended reads, a poetry glossary and our blog.

If you would like to order further copies of this book,
or any of our other titles, then please give us
a call or visit **www.youngwriters.co.uk**.

Young Writers
Remus House
Coltsfoot Drive
Peterborough
PE2 9BF
(01733) 890066
info@youngwriters.co.uk